DATE DUE

COUNSEL ON APPEAL

COUNSEL

Lectures on appellate advocacy sponsored
by the Committee on Post-Admission
Legal Education of The Association of
the Bar of the City of New York

 McGRAW-HILL BOOK COMPANY
New York   San Francisco   Toronto   London   Sydney

CHARLES D. BREITEL

SAMUEL E. GATES

WHITMAN KNAPP

THURGOOD MARSHALL

ON APPEAL

MILTON POLLACK

SIMON H. RIFKIND

HARRIS B. STEINBERG

Arthur A. Charpentier EDITOR

COUNSEL ON APPEAL

02402

1234567890 VBVB 7543210698

INTRODUCTION

". . . it is the fish that the angler is after
and all his recondite learning is but the
hopeful means to that end."   JOHN W.
DAVIS, *The Argument of an Appeal*

When John W. Davis, surely the leading
advocate of his time, drew this piscatorial analogy in 1940
he had in mind the great need which he had observed
for advocates to study carefully the process of presenting
questions of law and social policy to appellate courts so
that it would be both enjoyable and productive.

That this process went beyond the mere mechanics of
presentation into the rationale of the entire exercise became quite evident as Mr. Davis unfolded his lecture,
now a treasured classic of the bar. Twenty-eight years later,
there now follows this volume containing contributions by
a group of contemporary experts, as a sort of response. The
project was mainly conceived and presented under the
guidance of a leading and most imaginative jurist, Hon.
Charles D. Breitel, who has just been elected, almost unanimously, to New York's highest court.

John W. Davis rather thought that it was the judicial fish who might best introduce the advocate angler to the deeper pools where rises come and provide guidance as to the best lures. But Judge Breitel has generally preferred to treat his advocate colleagues, like Mr. Davis himself, as the best guides to the mysteries of the advocate's tackle box.

Judge Breitel was also conscious that since the days of Davis too little had been heard from the thoughtful, successful advocate of today; that there had been more than enough concern with mechanics and technique and too little exploration of the emotional and philosophic requirements of the forum.

Accordingly, he drafted a group of outstanding practitioners of appellate advocacy. He asked them to consider aloud the climate of their work, the ends to be achieved within the appellate structure—to create, in words, the colors and emotions to which they addressed themselves and, finally, to dissect their responses to the needs which they felt.

The result is this series of lectures, each in its own way adding a fresh dimension of understanding to the appellate process. The lecturers recognize differences in courts, in advocates, in issues, and in clients. One of the most interesting things which emerges is the fundamental and common integrity of purpose which ultimately unites advocate and court in the search for truth amid conflict, forging the rule of law and many of the standards of fairness and honor which govern conduct in each generation.

The selection of lecturers was ingenious. All of them, of course, had high qualifications as outstanding appellate advocates. Each was generally specially experienced in a somewhat different field from the others. Two of them, former District Judge Simon Rifkind and Solicitor General, now Mr. Justice, Thurgood Marshall, as Judge Breitel, the Chairman, had observed the problems and participated notably in the process from both sides of the bench. Another, Milton Pollack, a leader particularly of the equity trial and appellate bar, has been appointed a Judge of the Southern District since his lecture was given. Harris Steinberg is recognized as probably the leading silk at the criminal bar of New York today. Whitman Knapp had broad experience both as prosecutor and private counsel. Samuel Gates is an experienced trial and appellate advocate with broad experience both in courts and administrative tribunals.

So Judge Breitel has brought about a most productive and unusual combination—both fish and angler searching together for the nature of the goal and the lure. While he has properly emphasized, as he set out to do, the advocate, the infusion of the judicial mystique, with its often obscure trade secrets, has given these lectures a well-rounded quality which other efforts have often lacked.

What emerges is a fascinating study of motivation and efforts as appellate courts strive to resolve those enigmas which advocates seek to explain. One rises from reading the lectures with a strong feeling that advocate and judge take great joy and satisfaction in the routine and responsibility of their tasks. And they indicate that there is also joy in the flash and sparkle which brings life and color to the stream and inspires the advocate to his most adventurous casts. No day spent in the courthouse in such an excit-

ing activity is ever begrudged or forgotten by the participants.

Arthur A. Charpentier, the outstanding former librarian
of The Association of the Bar and a warm friend of its
members, now the librarian of the Yale Law School, has
provided valuable help in preparing these lectures for
publication.

Whitney North Seymour

PREFACE

The Committee on Post Admission Legal Education of The Association of the Bar of the City of New York sponsors, in the course of the average year, an extensive program of lectures and forums in every conceivable area of interest to the bar. No series held during the past few years attracted more interest than did the lectures on appellate advocacy published in this volume.

Both E. Nobles Lowe, chairman of the Committee on Post Admission Legal Education and Judge Charles D. Breitel, who conceived and organized the lectures, were very pleased when the McGraw-Hill Book Company expressed interest in their publication.

The lectures are published in the order in which they were delivered. Leading references to cases and materials made by the various speakers have been identified and listed at the end of each published lecture. I have edited the discussion which followed each published lecture into a question and answer format without identifying inquirers by name.

Editing this volume has been a pleasure for me for many

reasons. The lecturers themselves have been most helpful, in particular Whitman Knapp, who represented the very busy Judge Breitel, in arranging many of the publishing details. Finally, another cubit has been added to the debt I owe Paul B. DeWitt, Executive Secretary of The Association of the Bar of the City of New York; a valued friend of many years.

ARTHUR A. CHARPENTIER
Yale Law School

CONTENTS

The Criminal Appeal

HARRIS B. STEINBERG

Harris B. Steinberg, a former vice-president of The Association of the Bar, has served as chairman of its Executive Committee and in numerous other capacities within the association. He is a graduate of the Harvard Law School and a fellow of the American College of Trial Lawyers. He is a member of the National Association of Defense Lawyers in Criminal Cases. He has served as an assistant district attorney in New York County (1938–1942) and as a special assistant attorney general of the state of New York. He is a member of the bars of New York State, the Federal Courts in the Second Circuit, and the United States Supreme Court. He is a specialist in the conduct of criminal cases.

Most of us, I am sure, have experienced those distressing dreams in which we find ourselves inadequately clothed, in some public place, experiencing agonies of embarrassment. Tonight it is borne in on me that my situation is very much like that. Admittedly I must bear a large measure of the blame for permitting myself to be held out as having something significant to say to you about criminal appeals. But what gives me a particularly unclothed feeling and makes the experience an unsettling one is that I see in the audience a number of people who, by virtue of their being appellate court judges, former colleagues or former adversaries, have a great store of knowledge, not only about the broad aspects of criminal appeals but about the humiliating details of how I learned my lessons in that field. For, in this case as in most others in the law, the really worthwhile lessons are those learned through one's mistakes and defeats, and when it comes to mistakes and defeats, I will match my record against any man's.

Since this is the first lecture in a series, I think it would be well to state that neither the series nor this part of it is conceived as a discussion of techniques or as embodying suggestions on how to persuade an appellate court to one's position.

It is clear that the task of persuading an appellate tribunal of the justice of a criminal defendant's plaint is essentially a highly individual and creative one. It is not hyperbole to denominate it as an art. Today when so much that is accepted as art encompasses elements from the everyday world of comic strips and junk, as well as elements of applied science and the skills of the eye doctor, the simile is even more valid. If one accepts this premise, it is easy to understand why, once the painter has stretched his canvas and placed it on the easel, it is no help to him to be told to dip his brush in red paint as opposed to black or to make a broad, heavy stroke instead of a delicate one. There can be no valid qualitative comparison of two widely different concepts of how a picture should look, so long as both are the sincere products of a true artist. It is only the amateurish, the bogus, and the mass-produced product designed for the marketplace rather than for the soul which can be summarily discarded. For the rest, the proper criterion, it seems to me, is whether the effort is so conceived that it is reasonably calculated to achieve its objective and whether the artist or actor attorns to, and is in harmony with, the broad objectives of the system of which he seeks to be an effective and cooperative part.

Our aim is to try to isolate and examine, if possible, those aspects of the criminal appeal process of which a lawyer must be aware so that he can direct his individual talents and skills toward persuasion with the maximum chance of success that his case merits. If we can only glimpse these elements, even as if through a glass, darkly, each lawyer, each individual artist, will know surely and instinctively how his own particular talents, whether for the use of strident areas of strong color or for subtle harmonies of delicate tone, can best be used to paint his own picture.

In an effort to establish a jumping-off place for tonight's discussion, I sought some statistics about an appellant's chances for reversal in a criminal appeal. On the federal side, these figures were not easily uncovered by the kind of desultory and dispirited research I am in the habit of conducting. However, informed guesses from the Second Circuit were to the effect that not more than one criminal appeal in fifteen, perhaps, is successful.

On the state side, an obliging assistant district attorney in the Appeals Bureau of the New York County Office took the trouble to dig up for me the following figures. In cases handled by that bureau in the Court of Appeals during 1965, there were 27 outright affirmances and 6 affirmances with some modification, while there were only 4 reversals. In cases in the Appellate Division, First Department, there were 159 outright affirmances and 2 additional affirmances with modification, while there were only 7 reversals. In cases handled by that office in the Appellate Term, First Department, there were 121 outright affirmances and 7 more with some modification, while the reversals numbered only 8.

These figures, more graphically than anything else, give us an insight into the true situation of an appellant in a criminal case. To put it mildly, it is an uphill fight and, I strongly suspect, much more of an uphill fight than one encounters in a civil appeal. Some of the reasons for this difference would seem to be readily apparent, but I shall await with interest the detailed discussion on that topic by Whitman Knapp in the third lecture of this series.

I remember a cartoon in *Punch* that struck a responsive chord in me when I saw it. It depicted a large stone cell, with heavily barred and inaccessible windows high on the wall. The door was a massive one, with iron spikes em-

bedded in it. In the middle of the bare room, two emaci-
ated, bearded, and ragged men hung suspended from the
ceiling by chains. Their hands were manacled behind their
backs, and their legs were chained to huge iron balls. Their
situation was about as hopeless as the artist could depict it.
But one man was whispering to the other, "Now, here is
my plan!" As long as we have such indomitable and opti-
mistic responses to the adversities experienced by defendants, we shall have criminal appeals. I suspect, also, that we
shall continue to have roughly the same number of reversals as there are escapes from the barred cell depicted
in *Punch*.

The sobering statistics which I have just put before you
tell us something else, it seems to me, about the real nature
of the adversary faced by the appellant's lawyer. With all
respect to the able advocates who people the appeals bu-
reaus of the prosecution offices, I suggest that the principal
opponent to be overcome is the court itself, with its instinctive desire to hold firm the bastions of organized society
against harmful and antisocial conduct. The court is not,
as in a civil case, merely an arbiter between two equal com-
batants in a dispute in which society has very little stake.
In a criminal case the court is alert to recognize that, however well or ineptly the lawyer for the People of the State of
New York or the lawyer for the United States of America
does his job, it is incumbent on the court to subject the appellant's points to the court's own careful scrutiny and
to weigh them in the light of the knowledge that its only
choice is to affirm or to reverse. The ineluctable nature of
the duty enforced on the court means that a decision
that a serious error has been made below will free the
defendant. Surely a judge cannot help but experience at

least a modicum of distress that he should be the cause of a dangerous person's being set at large. The position was articulated at its baldest by a French scholar, who commented on the English criminal-appeal system in the eighteenth century as follows, according to Professor Radzinovicz, in his *History of English Criminal Law:*

> LeBlanc, referring to the trial for high treason of a certain Christopher Layer, quotes the exceptions brought forward by the defence, which were that whereas the name of the accused was Christoporus, the indictment spoke of Christop*her*us, and that one or two sentences in the indictment were expressed in incorrect Latin. On this he comments: "Can one seriously hear such discussions of insignificant grammatical niceties, in an affair of such importance? . . . After all, is it not as if the Counsellor had said: the prisoner, whose defence is committed to me, may be a traytor to his country, but his prosecutors are guilty of blunders, contrary to the rules of the Latin grammar; for which reason, I demand that he be set at liberty, tho' his crime enormous as it is, go unpunish'd."

Of course, we all know that the English judges were cognizant of a significant fact which apparently eluded the indignant French scholar: the savagery of the English criminal law of that period, which numbered more than 200 capital offenses and which carried out those penalties with unexampled cruelty, could not but sadden a humane man. Children of the tenderest years were executed for mere peccadilloes, and executions were carried out in public by hanging, burning, boiling, beheading, hanging in chains, and drawing and quartering. Judges, too, are human, and if correcting Latin grammatical errors appears to be a useful way to avoid boiling a curly-headed ten-year-old who stole sixpence, it is no wonder that the appellate courts of several centuries ago were willing to mask their real reasons for acting as they did with a solemn false face of hypertechnicality. At any rate, I believe we can find evidence in support of the proposition that in a criminal appeal, despite the forms, the appellant's real adversary is the court's reluctance to take a step which has the necessary practical effect of setting at liberty a man who has done dangerous and destructive things.

First, there are the statistics themselves. The assistant district attorneys may indeed be good lawyers, but they just can't be *that* good. Indeed, when they enter private practice, they usually find that they, too, fall prey to the same statistics which they sometimes cite in their annual reports. I recall that my former chief and mentor in the Appeals Bureau of the New York District Attorney's Office, Stanley Fuld, now chief judge of the Court of Appeals,[1] long ago gave it as his opinion that more than 80 percent of the criminal appeals would be affirmed even if only a token brief were submitted by the People.

I surely do not wish to be understood as minimizing the importance of the contribution that the respondent's attorney makes to the complement of court and counsel in a criminal appeal. I think merely that in order to understand the true dynamics of the situation it is sufficient to concentrate on the show in the center ring—the duel between the appellant's lawyer and the court's conscience—and it is not necessary to consider the responses of the prosecutor. The latter's responses, of necessity, are primarily a scrutiny and

[1] On the date when the lecture was delivered, Judge Fuld was an associate judge. He has since been elected chief judge.

testing of the validity of the appellant's position, of essentially the same sort which the court itself makes and which, indeed, the appellant has himself long since made if he is to be taken at all seriously. The only thing I will say in this regard is that the most devastating kind of respondent's lawyer an appellant can face is one who is consummately fair. If the court feels that the prosecutor also wishes a just result, it will place more reliance on the exposition of difficulties in the way of reversal which the prosecutor will deftly spread before it. It is in the relatively few cases marked by close divisions in the decisions that this role of the prosecutor will most often make itself felt.

Second, there are the interesting things that happen when a prosecutor tries to confess error. One of my early recollections at the bar is of a case handled by Felix Benvenga, another of my former chiefs in the same Appeals Bureau. Convinced that a serious error had been committed at the trial, he stated in his brief that he agreed with the appellant's position and declared his consent to reversal. The Appellate Division, First Department, despite this well-meant display of objectivity, affirmed the conviction and made it quite clear that in future it desired nothing from the advocates but advocacy, rather than advice or a usurpation of the judicial function of *deciding cases*. There is, of course, a significant difference between candidly admitting error, while arguing as to its effect, and agreeing to a reversal. Recently, in the course of the vague and pottering kind of research that I sporadically conduct, I asked one of the clerks in the Court of Appeals in Albany what information he had about attempts by prosecutors to confess reversible error in that court. He told me that in his many years of observation he could recall about six such instances: in four of them the court had affirmed the convictions, despite the prosecutors' attempts to consent to reversal. Certainly such a result is rarely to be expected in a civil case. In civil cases, if counsel for both sides agree on a disposition satisfactory to them, it would hardly occur to the court to thwart their common desires, except in the rarest of cases. An example of such a rare case, *Alton v Alton*, did arise in the Third Circuit. It involved the validity of a Virgin Islands divorce. The court, of its own motion and in the face of objections from both litigants, struck down the Virgin Islands divorce law. Of course, it acted from a concern for the public interest, which was not adequately represented by either litigant, and it did not feel that it should be bound by the litigants' position. In criminal cases, such an approach seems to be the rule rather than the exception.

In addition to the court's regarding itself as a protection for organized society against harmful incursions, there are several other factors that add weight and immobility to its initial posture of generalized inertia against reversal. One is a natural reluctance to change the particular result in the particular case, because that result has occurred in a trial court that is a part of the same integrated piece of legal machinery of which the appellate court is itself a part. Thus, for example, in the federal system appellate court judges use the same building and lunchrooms as trial judges, lunch daily with their brethren of the trial bench, meet them socially, confer with them at judicial conferences, and enjoy many opportunities to assess them as decent, able, and dedicated colleagues and friends. Will not such a judge experience at least an involuntary pang when he finds it incumbent on him to reverse his brother of the nisi prius court and to lecture him publicly on his errors of law or judicial behavior? Even when he faces up to his duty with resolution, as I am sure all of them do, it does take an affirmative effort to move away from the *status quo*, whereas voting for an affirmance is psychologically an easier thing to do.

Another psychological deterrent against reversal of the court below in criminal cases is the impact of the inordinate public and newspaper interest in crime and sensational cases. We recall, with heartfelt and warm sympathy and distress, the wild-eyed pickets who chanted "Impeach Earl Warren" when the Chief Justice became an honorary member of this association a few years ago. No one doubts that that great man and his colleagues are not to be swayed by such mindless attacks, but can we be equally sure that as we get farther and farther down the rungs of the judicial ladder, into courts where the tenure is not so lengthy or so certain and into localities where passions run high, that every appellate judge who has to cast a vote in a sensational criminal case will be free from the subconscious desire to avoid a result which will subject him to abuse, vilification, or reprisal at the polls at the hands of the uninformed? For the most part the reversal of a conviction of a notorious or bad person will be a vindication of an abstract principle, hard for the lay public to grasp. That public, however, will be quick to appreciate that the most immediate beneficiary of the decision will be the unpopular and unworthy defendant and others similarly situated. Witness the current furore over the *Escobedo* and *Miranda* cases.

An additional factor inhibiting reversals is the very human one that the type of men—intellectual and experienced—who sit on our appellate courts cannot be expected to enjoy being lectured as to what they ought to do by lawyers who seek reversals. Whether the appellant's lawyer is a noble advocate, firmly advancing his arguments, or a cringing apologist, or something in between, his role is essentially a didactic one. Pupils, especially those who feel, with a good deal of justice, that they know as much or more than the volunteer teacher, are apt to become restive.

I have a clear recollection of the very first appellate argument I ever made. When Thomas E. Dewey was elected district attorney, virtually the entire office was restaffed and there was a monumental scurrying on January 1, 1938. As one of the youngest and surely the most inexperienced of the new assistants, I was assigned to the Appeals Bureau and told that I was to argue a case in the Appellate Division, First Department, on the very next day. The brief for the respondent had been written by a predecessor who was no longer on the staff. I feverishly read and reread the briefs, digested the cases cited, and committed the record to memory in the course of a sleepless night. Next day, red-eyed but informed, I made ready to argue. The prosecution brief had been written in a style then current, with a clean-cut division into two parts—first, "The Facts," and second, "The Law." This seemed perfectly logical to me, fresh as I was from arguments in the moot court competition at my law school, where the same style prevailed. Accordingly, I parroted off a close paraphrase of the facts that appeared in the brief and then, after a significant pause, announced portentously, "Now, your Honors, I come to the law."

With a smile, Presiding Justice Martin said, "Thank you, young man, but you may sit down; we know the law." I sat down hurriedly. I may say that that was a lesson I never forgot. Ever since, I have made careful efforts to argue and brief my cases so that when the record *facts* are discussed and made known in all their significant aspects, the law will automatically click into place without being heralded as an entity separate from my case.

These, then, are some of the factors that make for resistance to reversal on the court's part. If I may pursue my artistic analogies for a moment, the appellate court is like a heavy bronze statue resting on a marble plinth. Its weight makes it resistant to being toppled over. But if the marble base is rounded and shaped like a hemisphere, the statue will rock when it is pushed. With a strong enough push one may topple it in the direction desired by the pusher. The figurative roundness, or unsteadiness, of the base, which makes it subject to being toppled on occasion, is a fanciful way of describing the court's determination to do justice. This desire of the court to be an instrument of justice may seem so obvious as hardly to bear talking about, but I think it merits some consideration.

A *generalized* desire to do justice is an abstract feeling, and one may take it for granted, for the most part, as a mild, benevolent feeling of goodwill, having no practical effects. Some people may be more continually aware of it than others, but essentially it adds weight to the immobility we spoke of. But the desire to do justice springs sharply into our awareness when we are presented with a claimed instance of injustice. When the late Prof. Edmond Cahn examined the question of justice in the light of

The Sense of Injustice, he made a great contribution to legal philosophy and aided our understanding of the legal process immeasurably. We can be sure that no judge on any appellate court would willingly permit his vote in any case to be used to perpetrate or continue an *injustice*. Understanding this, the appellant does not come to the court seeking abstract justice, but he complains that he is the victim of *injustice*, in the form of a specific violation of his substantial rights. One can only right an injustice by doing something about it. This sense of injustice starts a rocking motion when it is properly conveyed.

What gives the search for justice a most fascinating interest is the set of formalized rules and concepts, unique to our system, within which lawyers and judges act. These rules are not always conducive to ascertaining the "truth" as an objective fact, but the courts are as much, or more, interested in maintaining certain important civilized values as they are in getting at the truth.

Dean Thayer of Harvard Law School, many years ago, wrote:

> In dealing with litigation courts are not engaged in an academic exercise; with them the search for truth is not the main matter. Their desire to know this and their ability to use it are limited by the requirements of their *main* business, that of awarding justice.

Typical of rules that promote justice, at the expense of getting at the objective truth, are the exclusion of wiretapping evidence and the refusal to accept evidence that is the result of an undue delay in arraignment or the result of an unlawful search and seizure.

Most criminal cases, when they appear on the appellate

scene, have a seductive black-and-white simplicity. The arrest was made by vigilant police, the indictment was returned by twenty-three grand jurors, the trial evidence proved the defendant guilty beyond a reasonable doubt, and the jury's verdict, unanimous and decisive, for all practical purposes took the factual questions out of the realm of controversy. What is there left except to set at rest some hindsight claims that a mistake was made, in some manner, in this lengthy and complicated process, all of which has been laboriously set up and expensively administered to make sure that the innocent shall not be wrongly convicted? When the appellant's points are presented, the appellate court's generalized desire to be just and fair is covered by a horny layer of callus developed over the years by hearing many such claims in the past, most of which turned out to be embarrassingly unfounded. A gloomy feeling, all but a certainty, pervades the court: it is to the effect that there is little left but to affirm. The first part of the advocate's job is to make the court feel that there is a reasonable and arguably sound alternative to the familiar probabilities. He must make clear that there is a real choice in the case. Widening the court's choice of action is a creative job for the advocate. He seeks thereby to encourage in the first place a state of imbalance or indecision which I prefer to call open-mindedness, and then— and only then—does he sound the siren call to take a practical and correct way out of the dilemma, in order to solve the difficulty which he has exposed to the court's view.

This creative job is helped by the fact that there are many alternative legal rubrics under which a single set of facts can be considered. The finding of the blind men in

India who touched the elephant to learn what it was like are analogous to the myriad choices that suggest themselves to the advocate who seeks a handle and a traditional label under which to categorize and identify, in familiar terms, his plea for justice. You will recall that one blind man touched the elephant on the trunk and concluded that elephants are all like snakes, while another felt the leg and opined that the nature of the beasts was more like that of tree trunks, while the one who touched the tail gave it as his opinion that elephants were like ropes, and so on. The lawyer who sees the case whole and senses an injustice that merits redress will brood over his record, sort out the decisions and statutes in his own jurisdiction, sift the most recent cases from Washington, and ponder as to which organ of the elephant is most appropriate for description to the court. He knows that whether he calls it a rope or a tree trunk or a snake, the court is more likely to recognize it for what it really is—part of a whole beast—but once he can persuade the court at least to start feeling the beast in cooperation with him, something good will result from their partnership in applied zoology.

Professor Cahn, in his book *The Moral Decision*, stated the function of the advocate with lucid insight:

> We discover our decision by means of confronting the alternatives, well enough; but this process, if confined to a single psyche, may become so entangled in the conflicts of competing subjective impulses that often nothing results but confused indecision. Endless debate with one's self can lead to a state of inanition—the inner forces come so nearly in balance that none seems capable of forming a decisive structure.
>
> What occurs to catalyze the process is very simple and

familiar. Some other person is asked to express a choice. He or she does. Forthwith, the inner structure falls into shape, in direct or inverse response to the other's presentation. The advocate outside has accomplished what the contending voices within had failed to do—he has won the case or has unwittingly exposed all its weakness. The choice I hear from outside I know is mine, or I know is not mine. In any case, once I have heard it, I feel certain I know.

Occasionally an exasperated prosecutor will complain to an appellant's lawyer, as they withdraw from the courtroom after an argument. "You weren't logical; you jumped back and forth between the law and the equities, and you never stuck to one or the other." This is a fair comment and fairly describes what must necessarily be an important part of the appellant's technique. If any case were clearly in favor of the defendant, in all likelihood he never would have been indicted and tried. And if he were completely deserving of sympathy and had not done something wrong and bad, the prosecutor or the grand jury would probably have aborted the prosecution early in the proceedings. But the skill of the appellant's lawyer is in tracing a path to freedom for his client, which sometimes requires nimble jumping from stone to stone across the brook in zigzag fashion, from the "justice" or "equity" stones to the "law" or "fact" stones and back, rather than along one straight line.

Jesting Pilate propounded a query not easily to be answered when he asked, "What is truth?" It is not always a single and indivisible whole. There is more than one truth to be discerned. The late Mr. Justice Frankfurter, in *Of Law and Men*, wrote as follows:

"But when, in any field of human observation, two truths appear in conflict it is wiser to assume that neither is exclusive, and that their contradiction, though it may be hard to bear, is part of the mystery of things." . . . But judges cannot leave such contradictions between two conflicting "truths" as "part of the mystery of things." They have to adjudicate. If the conflict cannot be resolved, the task of the Court is to arrive at an accommodation of the contending claims. This is the core of the difficulties and misunderstandings about the judicial process. This, for any conscientious judge, is the agony of his duty.

Judges who continually face their "agony of duty" learn, after years on the bench, that a fair or reasonable admixture of law, facts, equities, civilizing values, and an open heart is all that can ever be expected to emerge from the appellant's side. If that is to be rejected as insufficient because it is impossible to put "Q.E.D." after it, one may as well do away with the entire process of appeals.

The ways in which a court discerns the right decision are not always those suggested by the advocate. Sometimes the court indulges its own creative instincts, to the advantage or disadvantage of the appellant. For example, in 1913, the New York Court of Appeals had before it *People v Cummins*. The case was one that had excited a great deal of acrimony against the defendant because it involved the failure of a bank in which many depositors had lost a good deal of money. The defense was conducted by the late Max Steuer. The defendant was convicted, and that judgment was affirmed in the Appellate Division. In the Court of Appeals the judgment was again affirmed. A very able judge, Willard Bartlett, wrote the opinion and, as was customary in those days, dealt separately and at length with each of the many points raised. The determined and methodical knocking down in turn of each of the many ingenious and, in some cases, serious points was like the inexorable progress of a tank through a street of flimsy huts. The key to the result, of course, was in the concluding words of the opinion:

> Notwithstanding the complicated mass of proof in this case and the devious paths in which the evidence was occasionally permitted to stray, I am satisfied after a very careful study of the long record, that the minds of the jurors were clearly directed to the true issues involved, that they were not misled or confused to the detriment of the defendant, and that the case presents no legal error which would justify this court in interfering with the verdict.

Readers of the reported opinion must admire the single-minded manner in which the unanimous court came to this practical conclusion, although they may experience a vicarious feeling of strain when they come to this portion of the opinion, which dealt with a claim of error in the admission of evidence:

> The only objection was to the materiality and relevancy of this evidence, save in a single instance where the constitutional ground was specified and the objection was then sustained. It is suggested that counsel for the defendant upon the trial were prevented from specifying the constitutional objection to this evidence by a ruling of the learned trial judge during the defendant's cross-examination, after the court had overruled an objection to a question put by the assistant district attorney. This appears in the record as follows:
>
> MR. STEUER: Just pardon me a second.
> THE COURT: You have got my ruling.
> MR. STEUER: May I not state my objection? If you do

not want me to, I am perfectly satisfied to abstain.

THE COURT: After all, Mr. Steuer, in a criminal case it is not necessary to state at length the ground of your objection.

MR. STEUER: I understood, your Honor, that rule applied only to a case where a man was being tried for murder in the first degree.

THE COURT: It applies to every case.

MR. STEUER: I do not understand that you could argue an appeal without an exception.

THE COURT: I am not talking about an exception. I am speaking of the grounds of the objection. It is not necessary to state the grounds of the objection. You stated your objection and I overruled it.

MR. STEUER: I really did not know that.

The learned trial judge inadvertently erred in this expression of opinion. While it is true that the grounds of an objection should not be stated at inordinate length, they should be clearly and fully specified to make the objection available on appeal.

Another route to a similar destination was taken by the United States Supreme Court, in *Mapp v Ohio*. There, as you all know, the Court was concerned with an unlawful search and seizure of certain incriminating evidence and its use in a state court prosecution. The Ohio court had followed the rule, prevailing in New York and many other jurisdictions, permitting the use of evidence obtained in that manner if it was otherwise relevant and material. Counsel for the appellant in the Supreme Court was arguing with the discouraging knowledge that he was flying in the face of the long-established rule, which a majority of the states had adopted and which had been repeatedly accepted by the Supreme Court in the past. One of the justices leaned forward and asked, "Aren't you asking us to overrule *Wolf v Colorado,* counsel?" The lawyer is reported to have replied, "I am sorry, your Honor, but I am not familiar with that case." The *Wolf* case, of course, was the principal obstacle to the appeal. What happened is history. The Supreme Court did reverse in *Mapp,* and in the course of its opinion, and indeed as an indispensable part of the tidying process necessary for that task, it overruled its own prior decision in *Wolf v Colorado.*

Is it not also relevant to our discussion to consider what sort of man an appellate lawyer in criminal cases should be, to be effective? When we spoke of persuading the court, we used the figure of speech of toppling a bronze statue. But is not the court likely to resist more strongly a push by a hand that it suspects to be unclean? Can one talk in terms of abstract principles of justice, of what is fair or unfair, and carry conviction if the court has heard rumors or made its own appraisals, based on past experiences with disingenuous and misleading briefs, and finds the advocate to be an unworthy person? The erring minister says, "Don't do as I do; do as I say." But the congregation is more likely to follow his exhortations if they can feel that they are being asked to do not only what the minister says but what he does. In a real sense, I believe, the character of an appellate lawyer in a criminal case is a palpable factor in the court's response to his urgings.

We are fortunate in this country and especially in this city in that we are a melting pot of many cultures and races. Lawyers who grew up in neighborhoods where some of their schoolmates were destined for the electric chair while others became respected citizens; lawyers who, as

children, heard from the lips of their parents tales of
pogroms and brutality by police officials of other lands;
lawyers who come from families that suffered harsh in-
dignities because of race or religion; lawyers whose fathers
and mothers, deprived of schooling, were consumed with a
thirsty passion that their children should be learned, wise,
and just; and lawyers who trace their ancestry back to
Revolutionary days, when their forebears risked their lives
and fortunes in fighting for our independence—and the
Constitution: all these are to be found among those admitted to practice here. It is too bad that more of these
intangible riches of our bar, in idealism and talent, are
not available on the criminal side.

In decades past, there were many respected and able
advocates who functioned with equal ease in both civil
and criminal cases. James Johnson of Philadelphia, Harold
Medina, Lloyd Paul Stryker, John McKim Minton, Max
Steuer, and many others come to mind. The gradual
abdication of the criminal side by men of this stripe has
left a very small number of advocates who, by virtue of
scholarship, standing at the bar, reputation, and character,
are equal to the task of elucidating, and in some measure
standing as symbols of, the great moral issues presented
by criminal cases. Until recently the ablest young lawyers
have not found it professionally or economically desirable
to enlist on that side of the appellate and trial bar. Fortunately, of late there seems to be an increased interest
in criminal law, which has been accelerated by the developments springing from the decision in *Gideon v Wain-*

wright. Legal Aid lawyers, volunteers, and assigned counsel are bringing their skill, imagination, and idealism to criminal appeals, and the beneficent results are growing more apparent every day.

It is interesting that members of this new generation of able lawyers, intrigued by the exciting developments in the Supreme Court, are dealing thoroughly with constitutional issues; but it is noticeable that they never seem to find evidentiary questions. Today there is hardly a claim of error on appeal that turns on the erroneous exclusion or admission of evidence. One reason is that the art or science of the law of evidence is dying out with an earlier generation of lawyers. Harvard Law School, for example, no longer requires a course in evidence as a prerequisite for graduation. For another thing, the growth of administrative bodies, with permissive rules as to hearsay and Xerox copies and the shotgun modern version of the shopbook rule, has bred a generation of lawyers who do not find it necessary or profitable to pore over abstruse evidence rulings. The standard trial court rulings today are "I'll take it for what it's worth" and "Proceed, counsel."

Judge Cardozo, in *Law and Literature*, gave a good many helpful hints to the appellate lawyer, but I think the most cogent thing he said was his final injunction, "Above all, don't be long-winded." And so I close with this thought. The world of the criminal-appeal lawyer is the physically circumscribed one of the library, the courtroom, and the office. Its weapons are books and papers and the spoken word. But the contest waged is one for high stakes, and the exhilarating battles often require the same sort of courage we are accustomed to look for in more bruising forms of conflict.

This is so because, in a day when conformity and a numbing consensus of beliefs are putting a gray pall of sameness over our lives and stifling unorthodox opinion, the criminal-appeal lawyer is a voice of dissent. That this is a voice of respectful and constructive dissent is clear, because in framing his appeals he necessarily attorns to our system and the forms of law. He seeks redress within their framework, rather than by destructive and anarchic attacks hostile to our philosophy. He is worth nurturing and cherishing.

In short, the life of the appeal lawyer is one of excitement and high intellectual adventure. I feel greatly privileged that it has been my lot to pursue that life.

QUESTION PERIOD

QUESTION: In the selection of the trunk or the tail or the legs, would you advise appellant's counsel to ignore the rest of the beast and put on respondent's counsel the responsibility of reminding the court that the entire beast has quite a different shape from that which is portrayed in the appellant's briefs?

MR. STEINBERG: No. I think it would be unwise to leave so obvious a rejoinder. I think you can certainly say, and you don't have to say it in a loud voice or in a lengthy manner, "Of course there is this, that, or the other thing, but. . . ." I don't think you would want to put yourself in a position of concealing anything by stating your argument in such a fashion that it is not complete. The aim is to be so complete yourself as to make the rejoinder seem boring.

QUESTION: I would like to ask Mr. Steinberg how much weight he gives to oral argument.

MR. STEINBERG: I think anybody who submits his case isn't worthy of taking an appellate case.

The oral argument is a place to make a contact. It is a relationship of interchange, interplay. I can't help but feel that when I walk out after an argument, I have planted the kind of emotional feeling that I am going to get a chance, that the judge is going to read my brief with a feeling that it has got a patina on it of what I said.

QUESTION: I just wanted to make reference to those statistics on the great number of affirmances that Harris Steinberg mentioned. People may not be familiar with the kinds of appeals that there are these days and may not realize that many of the appeals come from the coram nobis applications by prisoners or are appeals on the suppression of evidence when the defendants have already pleaded guilty. Many of these petitions are prepared by the prisoners themselves.

MR. STEINBERG: Could you give us an estimate of substantive appeals, as distinguished from the scattered kind you spoke of? What are the statistics?

QUESTIONER: I don't have them, but you can guess from the number of completed trials in the Supreme Court.

JUDGE BREITEL: Even taking the substantive appeals alone, you would not get a pure statistic. With the present virtually absolute right to an appeal and the assignment of counsel, regardless of the preliminary showing of merit required under the old rule, any defendant in any criminal case who wishes to appeal can do so and have counsel assigned. This means that even a large number of substantive appeals have become largely *pro forma*, regardless of how able or astute the counsel are that may be assigned to them.

I don't know the gross numbers, but I would estimate roughly from examining appeals in our court that in any month we probably have twenty to thirty coram nobis appeals of which no more than two or three present a truly decidable question, and then during that same month there would be, I would suggest, twenty substantive appeals of which maybe one-fourth would present a decidable question.

QUESTION: You placed an appellate court judge in the role of a judicial advocate, and in that connection I would like to ask you what you conceive to be the justice of the rule, laid down particularly by the Federal Court of Appeals and the Supreme Court, that in reviewing a criminal record when a jury has found a verdict of guilty, the courts must construe all facts in favor of the prosecution? Have they polled the jurors? Have any appellate courts polled jurors in criminal cases to determine whether or not in fact they really determined all the issues on the basis of a review of all the evidence? Don't you and I know as trial lawyers that very often jurors find a verdict of guilty on some single isolated item of evidence?

Why should there be any such appellate presumption? What basis is there for it, and why should a man's guilt be determined on any such presumption?

MR. STEINBERG: Well, as I understand the question, if you are seeking an alliance with me on the ground that it is not really true that the jury has passed on questions of fact, I reject the alliance because I feel that whether it has or not is not important. I feel that our system of justice has somnific qualities to it, and necessarily so; because we don't have IBM machines, we can't deal with every case. We must accept the presumption as a symbol.

I am sure that a lot of things go on in jury rooms that are wrong and that juries very often ignore courts' instructions, but we as citizens of this country accept the fact that if you go through the forms with a minimum of avoidance of the forms, substantial justice will have been served in the broad spectrum. This is a problem in life. You have to go through the forms as though your wife is beautiful and you are rich. You have got to do the best you can with what you have.

QUESTION: I would like to ask Mr. Steinberg how in this state he would have defendants informed of their right to appeal and their right to have counsel assigned by the appellate court.

MR. STEINBERG: Well, that is done now. In assigned cases it is a rule of the court that they must be informed; you have to write a letter to them and get their signature, and a record is made very precisely. In fact, it sort of eggs them into appealing, I think.

QUESTION: I just wondered, Mr. Steinberg, whether the increasing volume of cases in recent years has made it tougher and tougher for you to get a reversal of a criminal conviction?

MR. STEINBERG: Everything is tough for me as I get older. But actually as you lose certain skills, you gain compensatory ones, and as you get older, I suppose you get more cases offered to you; and maybe I get cannier about selecting them. At any rate, I think our record of reversals has been rather better in recent years than before. But I don't know what to attribute it to.

QUESTION: Would you agree that in a criminal appeal the main bases of succeeding are principally the prejudicial conduct of the prosecutor and perhaps the prejudicial conduct and remarks of the judge? How would you emphasize these in your brief and in the oral argument?

MR. STEINBERG: I don't think there is any such thing as a main

basis. There are styles in prosecutors' actions, and I think you
must not try to torture a set of records into the likeness of a
set of facts it has nothing to do with. You must look at the
case and see what the record shows and what the merits are.

References Made by Mr. Steinberg

CASES

Alton *v* Alton (3d Cir 1953) 207 F2d 667
Escobedo *v* Illinois (1964) 378 US 478
Gideon *v* Wainwright (1963) 372 US 335
Mapp *v* Ohio (1961) 367 US 643
Miranda *v* Arizona (1965) 384 US 436
People *v* Cummins 1913) 209 NY 283, 103 NE 169
Wolf *v* Colorado (1949) 338 US 25

OTHER

Cahn, Edmond N., *The Moral Decision*, Indiana University Press,
    Bloomington, Ind., 1955, p. 271.
———, *The Sense of Injustice*, New York University Press, New York,
    1949.
Cardozo, Benjamin N., *Law and Literature*, Harcourt, Brace & Co.,
    New York, 1931.
Frankfurter, Felix, *Of Law and Men*, Harcourt, Brace & Co., New York,
    1956.
Radzinovicz, Leon, *A History of English Criminal Law*, Vol. 1, *The
    Movement for Reform*, Macmillan, New York, 1948.

The Civil Appeal

MILTON POLLACK

Milton Pollack, a member of The Association of
the Bar of the City of New York, the New York
County Lawyers' Association, and the New
York State Bar Association, received his legal
education at the Columbia Law School. He has
been admitted to the bar of the Courts of New
York State, the United States Supreme
Court, and various United States Courts
of Appeal and Federal District Courts.
He served as a director of the New York County
Lawyers' Association. He was recently appointed
judge of the United States District Court, Southern
District of New York.

In discussing the civil appeal, we are contending with an abstract and elusive subject. Unlike the confrontation of the facts of a particular civil appeal or even the confrontation of how to write a brief, the topic with which we must deal this evening is an amorphous concept, one from which the facts are removed. I find that the hardest part of such a subject is to get it started.

Judge Breitel has noted that appellate advocacy is some kind of fishing adventure in which the judge is something of a fish and the lawyer something of an angler. The speakers have been told to tell what kind of bait to hook these fish with. We were told in the opening of the series that each person in advocacy projects his own personality and that all advocates are different. But that comforting thought didn't help me very much in trying to prepare myself to explain what is involved in one's personality.

Harris Steinberg faced up to the task of explaining the criminal appeal and interestingly found that his principal opponent on the appeal was the court itself, which he said felt duty-bound to man society's bastions. In contrast and by way of providing a forum for me, he said that the advocate in the civil appeal gets off much more lightly because he faces only an arbiter between two advocates and the stakes are only money, not liberty or life. The case is not generally sprinkled with constitutional rights or fundamental rights and privileges.

I am going to suggest that the advocate in the civil

appeal has a more formidable task than does the advocate in the criminal appeal. We don't have any built-in advantages. There is no sensitive public reaction to a deprivation of money or property by a civil judgment, and rarely will fundamental human rights and constitutional guarantees be found in the enforcement and administration of the civil law. There are usually no personal liberties to be vindicated. The Bill of Rights rarely comes into our work.

When courts administer the law merchant, on corporate or tax matters, they generally have far fewer qualms about the harshness of a result if it happens to coincide with that magic predictability and symmetry of the law to which businessmen look for guidance.

The major assist that is furnished to the appellant by concern for personal liberties and rights makes it more likely that the advocate in the criminal appeal will touch a respondent chord that will undo the result below. Advocacy and briefs and arguments in civil appeals are placed under a more skeptical, stricter scrutiny for the establishment of reversible error.

I have not observed any important innovations in civil appeals, any scientific breakthrough or computerized method akin to the startling advances in the physical sciences during the past fifteen years. The design of the civil appeal has remained traditional. Machine-made answers have not yet intruded. There is, of course, a vast literature that is springing up pertinent to man and the machine in the search for law and justice, but it has not yet overtaken appeals.

Experience teaches that machines are always an adjunct

to human judgment. Their introduction usually develops from a search for means to save overhead. Initially they do. However, programming the machines, the key to any use of computers, is nonetheless a human job. Evaluation of facts and circumstances will, I predict, remain a human function tempered by human emotions, feelings, and perspectives. Computers can't be programmed for these.

It has been said on all sides that there is pressure for promptness in the judicial process, and that applies to appeals. A judge of a court of first instance, it is said, should be quick and courteous and wrong; wrong, because otherwise there would be nothing left for appellate courts to do. That might be the reason why we have civil appeals.

This, of course, brings on the thought that my talk could have been titled "The Civil Appeal—Why?" Perhaps we ought to examine the social need and justification of appeals at all. There is a recurrent drive by the courts and sometimes by the legislatures to limit appealable matter. There is a constitutional limitation in the case of the Court of Appeals. Why? Is it only because our courts are busy? And is there always a shortage of judges?

Maybe we don't need appeals. Historically they didn't exist. In Biblical times the children of Israel in the wilderness did without them. When Moses' father-in-law Jethro visited him in the wilderness and found him knocking himself out deciding cases, he suggested the appointment of judges to bear the load. Moses agreed and appointed judges. But he said, as you will find in your Bible if you take the trouble to look, "Bring the hard cases to me." He didn't say, mind you, "I'll review your decisions." Bring the hard cases to me in the first instance. Exodus 18:26 says: "The hard cases they brought unto Moses but every small matter they judged themselves."

Something like that was the practice in England and also in some of the Northeastern states. In the old days a justice of King's Bench or Common Pleas in England or, indeed, a trial judge in Massachusetts or New Hampshire could refer a case to the full court to rule on controlling principles of law. The trial would go on until a crucial legal question appeared. That question would be referred to, and resolved right then and there, by the full bench; then judgment proceeded and was entered in nisi prius. To the extent that we in New York can still bring a controversy on submitted facts before the Appellate Division as a court of first instance, we have a somewhat similar practice.

What are some of the objections to appeals? First, they are a large expense to the community. We have a highly expensive and costly device to deal with. There are court buildings to house judges, secretaries, clerks, attendants, and their supporting cast, all subsidized by the community.

Second, errors are the commodity of appeals. Everyone is presumed to know the law except judges who try cases; they have a Court of Appeals put over them to set them right. Law is the only profession in which the chances of errors are admitted to be so high that an elaborate machinery has been provided for their correction. The machinery, of course, also formulates policy on occasion. In other trades, to be wrong is regarded as a matter for regret. In the law alone is it regarded as a matter of course.

Third, most appeals are fruitless anyway. Perhaps we

ought to be reminded of the chances for success as they have been cataloged by the statistics. It becomes apparent that fewer than one-quarter of all civil appeals yield successful results for the appellant.

An examination of civil appeals in the United States Court of Appeals for the Second Circuit shows that over a recent three-year period the chances of obtaining a reversal in a civil appeal were only 17 to 21 percent. That statistic was derived from approximately five hundred civil appeals taken to the Second Circuit. Nationwide, the results of civil appeals in all federal circuits were fractionally better, but the expectancy for reversal in almost four thousand appeals over the same period was still under 25 percent.

The figures for civil appeals in the First Department, Appellate Division, do not seem to have been broken down, but *all* reversals in the First Department amounted to only 22 percent, with modifications in an additional 9 percent. It is not clear whether those modifications were significant or mere tinkering with the judgments below.

The results in the New York Court of Appeals for the fate of the civil appeal are equally dim on the average. Out of a total of 359 civil appeals, the affirmances were 271 and the reversals were 61, or 17 percent of the total, with 17 modifications recorded.

It is perfectly clear that in less than 20 percent of civil cases that go up on appeal has the advocate any influence on the case at all. Only in this small percentage are questions raised on which two different viewpoints are possible and equally acceptable from the juridical standpoint.

The appeal is an expensive luxury. With such a minor chance of success as has been indicated by the results, the venture into higher courts raises questions of the rationality of a litigant's judgment in authorizing an appeal.

The litigant requires lawyers, whose office associates, secretaries, clerks, and so on must be maintained or retained. He requires services of mechanical trades, such as printers, whose plants, equipment, and personnel must be created and subsidized. All of these must be supported on the search for the Golden Fleece. There should be no confusion by this reference to a fable. I refer, of course, to the quest for a favorable decision.

Appeals are really unnecessary because of two further reasons. First, the facts are rarely revised or even disputed on appeal. Every jury is told almost immediately that it is the sole judge of the facts. The trial proceeds that way, and it is rarely otherwise on appeal. Indeed, in the federal courts, the federal test, the "clearly erroneous" doctrine, rarely is applied in favor of an appellant. Second, on appeal credibility is rarely reviewed. Demeanor evidence has not been preserved by any sound tracks or any photography.

The state court review of the facts is similarly limited. If you were to examine state court cases over the last ten or fifteen years, you would find only a handful of cases that entire period in which an appellate court reversed on the weight of evidence. For all practical purposes, it may be said that when the facts have been found in the trial court, even in a state court, they are final.

Now, is there any reason for appeals because they help to make law? The legislature makes the law, and judges are not supposed to be lawmakers—at least, that's what they tell us.

If there were no appeals, trial judges faced with the

ultimate responsibility might exercise more care in the first instance, and so appeals have another reason for not being: they delay the ultimate determination of the civil controversy. The policy of the law is to terminate disputes quickly.

Then, too, the availability of the appellate procedure encourages its misuse. "All the ways of a man are right in his own eyes," says the Book of Proverbs. A dissatisfied litigant is only too glad to seek another court that he hopes will look at his ways as right, just as he looks at them as right, even though the trial court thought they were wrong.

Just let a litigant have enough money to afford an appeal and the appeal becomes a crusade. Unfortunately, some litigants who don't have the money to afford appeals insist on taking them. The really unfortunate situation is one in which the appellant has the money but the respondent hasn't.

The judges know what goes on, and from time to time some of them speak out about the waste involved. Court of Appeals Judge Jerome Frank once remarked, "The infirmities of the appeal are exceeded only by the hardihood of a plaintiff in taking it, but still they come." Theoretically the appellate courts can penalize unmeritorious cases, but they rarely do so.

Now let's turn to the other side of the coin. What are the arguments that favor the system of appeals? I suppose we could always start out with the phrase, "It is human to err," especially in overtaxed courts of first instance, and with the premise that it is civilized and sensible to remove error from civil conflict. Then, too, legal policy—not law-making but policy—has to be set, and trial courts really are not suited to making judicial policy. The existence of appeals has a great leavening influence on lower court judges. It makes them more conscious of duty through a responsiveness to legal criticism.

We know that redress of bad judicial decisions by legislation is slow and clumsy and that our entire system of government and philosophy of politics is one of checks and balances. It is, in the last analysis, a credit to the stability of our institutions that we are willing to subject their actions to the probing of appellate procedure. And even if we regard appellants as nothing more than devil's advocates, it says a great deal for a system of government that it allows even the devil to have his day in court.

Were we to take a poll of this audience or a voice vote or a show of hands, I wonder what the result would be. Are appeals here to stay? I think so. Accordingly, we have nothing left but to turn to the means of the appeal.

A civil appeal is definitely not an outlet for a desire to harass one's opponent, to increase one's remuneration, or even to gamble on favorable error at the hands of the higher court. The appellate advocate owes a duty to the profession to consider and proceed by honorable means consistent with the concepts and ends of justice.

Someone might well ask whether it is the function of an appellate advocate to censor the appeals brought to him on the ground that a client has a bad cause albeit a legal one. I suppose, as a matter of professional morals, if the lawyer acts with candor and without deception or misrepresentation and if he does no more than present the appeal in its most favorable light, he discharges his duty to himself, to his client, and to the ends of justice. Any other conclusion would mean that the lawyer must prejudge a cause by declining to undertake it. Were that to be the practice, the result would be that questionable cases would go without an advocate. If it was the duty of one, it would be the duty of all to abstain. That would result in an appeal's being decided before it got to court.

We constantly wonder what it is that produces success in the civil appeal. The work of the appellate advocate begins when he starts to locate the appealable subject matter and to organize a plan of presentation.

A plan is needed: a plan to force attention, create interest, and carry conviction on the selected subject matter. Without it, the job becomes a hopeless muddle in short order. The plan must take into account currents of thought—the temper of the times. It must even measure the philosophy and psychology of the individual judges and of the court as a whole.

Appellate advocacy on civil appeals calls for courage in the lawyer: the courage to forgo, the willingness to pass, alluring grounds that may exist in the record. The lawyer must make difficult choices. He must make calculated judgments in abandoning points for appeal. The compendious effort that throws everything erroneous or even everything reversible at the court runs the risk of pegging the strength of the appeal to the weakest link. Selectivity then is the key.

Paraphrasing the famous Mr. Dooley, we may say that the paramount issue for our side is the one the other side doesn't like to have mentioned.

The method of initial approach to the civil appeal varies, but if the case has been tried by others, it becomes essential to obtain not merely the information contained in the record but also an orientation right from the client. What it was that the client sought to have accomplished at the trial level must be determined. The trial judge's opinion, decision, and judgment and the briefs submitted to him must be read. It is only that type of comprehensive orientation which will lead you to what the case, in its true perspective, was all about.

What was the simple fact to have been decided, and what went wrong? Was the fact decided? Was it decided wrongly, and why? It is the simplification of each fact from an initial oriented approach that makes it possible to establish a plan of attack.

Each civil situation is susceptible of being painted and portrayed in living color, no matter whether it is corporate, tax, partnership, unfair competition, or one of the manifold other situations that develop and bring on civil appeals.

The aim of the advocate, of course, is to convince the court that he has a good case. Annually, Judge Breitel reminds the students at Columbia Law School, when he sums up moot court practice, that real courts deal with real cases but that in the moot court it is all fake. He tells them that in the moot court the advocate spends his time telling the court how good he is and how poor his case is. In real courts, on the contrary, he says that the lawyer devotes himself to proving how good his case is and to apologizing for how poor a lawyer he is. That inverse reasoning has often led me to wonder what happens when good lawyers show up in Judge Breitel's court? Are their cases judged accordingly, or else why did the good lawyers show up there?

In civil appeals, are appellate judges human beings? Is there any leavening influence, any humanizing influence? Have the judges become unemotional? Are they devoid of the human passions and reactions of lawyers and laymen? And are they devoid of an understanding of the human drama incident to the commercial and the tort situations? I don't think so. Experience teaches that sentiment has not fled from the civil appellate halls. There are many illustrations, particularly in the cases that involve interpersonal relationships.

To a greater or lesser extent it is true that all legal responses from civil judges and justices are conditioned by their own professional and lay experiences or even by the lack of them. Unquestionably, the desire of the civil appellate judge is to be just and to see that the right party wins. He desires further to make a contribution to good law and to create a legal heritage. It would be too much to suppose that he also seeks to reap the acclaim, let alone the applause, of the participants. However, none of the appellate judges with whom most of us have come in contact has ever failed in the endeavor to avoid giving offense or pain, and all judges in the higher courts desire to earn the respect and esteem of the members of the bar and of the public generally.

How do we go about persuading these judges on high? Style is a means of convincing. The wooing of the judicial mind ought to be conducted with confidence, with understatement, and with caution but with pungent directness and blunt expression, not with mere detached intellectualism.

It is almost the kiss of death, so far as I can make out,

to have overstuffed briefs and arguments relentlessly
crammed with minutiae and bogged down in repetitious
accounts. The best presentations are those that achieve
the greatest receptivity because they are more selective,
more concerned with the significance of the evidence, and
less concerned with a mere accumulation of the facts.

How about the reaction of the court to the advocate?
What are we able to observe from the judges' visible actions and reactions? There are those on the bench who
behave as though they were just silent spectators at a
sporting event and never react to the personality of the
lawyer who appears before them.

There are those who, given slight provocation or opportunity by an aggressive personality before them, take
on the role of a sparring partner and box away for the ex-
hilaration of the exercise. Sometimes, we see the judge
who, marking the appearance before him of what he thinks
is a dominant personality, feels impelled to step in to even
up the event by slugging the heavyweight to add to the
lightweight's presentation. That's a little hard to understand because although this tendency keeps the bar in
balance and assures against galloping ego, I wonder if it
aids in the objective consideration of a cause.

If we assume that the majority of the bench are the
quarry against which the appellate advocate must take aim
or the fish that must be lured, what kind of appellate advocacy will move the judges?

Perhaps it can be said that there are four kinds of
lawyers. There is the droll, happy lawyer with a bag full
of anecdotes. He hasn't been seen in the courthouse of
late, but he used to be there. This appellate advocate

provides entertainment that undoubtedly lightens the serious tasks. But we might ask: Do judges seek amusement? Are they really interested in a droll story while engaged in the serious business of administering justice?

Naturally, like all of us, they enjoy good quips and probably even good anecdotes, but after the mental applause meter has registered a high mark or even before that point has been reached, what then? Little remains on which a decision can be hung. That type of advocate doesn't seem to me to fulfill the appellate need. And that advocate will not provoke participation by the judge in the discussion of his case.

Then there is the sober, pedantic scholar. This appellate advocate, and you have all heard him, drones out a dry, intellectual exercise, pitched to educate and broaden the general knowledge of the judges. His polished, dry, unemotional presentation is likely to be received with an equally unemotional response. In all probability, judges feel no need for education on broad grounds as the basis for decision in specific civil cases. This type of advocate has a lulling effect rather than one that is provocative.

I recall the quip that made the rounds years ago when a lawyer said before Judge Shientag, "I make the usual motion, your Honor, to dismiss," and the judge responded, "I give you the usual answer—denied."

Then there is the fellow who comes into court with a personal grievance. He comes with a chip on his shoulder against his opponent and is ready to debate any judge who even intimates the acceptance of the opposition's argument. He is itching for a verbal quarrel.

Sometimes that advocate is met by a judge who rises to

the bait, accepts the challenge, and tilts and jousts to test his own skills at logic. This is really the court's advocate, who is addressing his colleagues through the punishment he is inflicting on the lawyer with his questions and answers.

That kind of advocacy is indeed provocative but may be of little help to the advocate. The combative style would seem not to be designed for persuasion; it easily can wind up on a discordant note.

Then there is the scared-rabbit type, the fellow who gets up at 2:05 and says, "I submit." He doesn't even come out of the hole but just seeks peace. He wants to be let alone. He assumes that the appellate judge wants to think quietly and without garrulous interruptions. That advocate misses the mark completely.

I have a candidate, and I'll tell you what my candidate is. He is different. I favor the lively, sparkling, assured type, the man who is out to sell his wares in a pleasant and, if you will, interested manner, the one who has found and can bring to life the human interest that his client has in the subject matter.

He knows the case that he is analyzing. He conveys with sincerity and earnestness the interesting facets of it and its relationship to affairs in the world in which we live and in which the case was born.

He will exude enthusiasm. His own sincere expression will become infectious, as happens whenever an empathy is created. He will, by his manner, move the judge to take hold of the case, examine it together with the advocate, and not merely be an outsider listening. What we all wish here is to involve the interest of the judge, to make of him a participant, if you will, in the hunt for the just and fair result and not merely an arbiter, aloof and detached.

Vigor and enthusiasm in the appellate advocate's presentation are more useful than overpolished and non-stimulating intellectualism as inducements for the judge to become a participant in the legal affray. It really is a court of men whom we are addressing and not an IBM machine, a cash register, or an adding machine taking note of the items on the register keys.

The organization of the effort to persuade the court necessarily must take into account the heavy burden that is being placed daily on the appellate courts by the proliferation of appeals. It becomes necessary almost to enable the judge to read or hear as he runs.

The advocate's job is to tell a quick-breaking story. He is dealing with real people and real problems, each of which had a substantial and human interest for the contestants. It is the re-creation of that human story which is the job of the advocate on the civil appeal. He must assume that the judge has never heard of the case or of his situation.

I venture to suggest that the most complicated civil matter, whether it is corporate, tax, probate, or any other, can and must be reduced to interesting simplicity. There is no such thing as a dry civil matter.

Too often on the civil appeal, the advocate becomes involved in a complex argument before he has told the basis of what happened, why it was wrong, and what relief he is seeking. Simplicity is vital in the art of persuasion.

The superstition that, once a court has allowed a precedent to live beyond its useful term, it is bound to continue the precedent's social security indefinitely unless an efficient legislature steps in to decree otherwise is philosophically a very troublesome doctrine. Inertia sometimes precludes judicial imagination and decision. Someone once wrote: "When laziness and timidity yoke us to our duties, we often give virtue the credit for it."

Are there any sure guideposts for success on the civil appeal? We have, as I have just indicated, the doctrine of *stare decisis*, and of that it is said that men are entitled, certainly at the civil law, to rely on the adherence of courts to established rules of law.

But what happens to *stare decisis* when it clashes with concepts of fairness and justice in the particular case? What has *stare decisis* to do with bringing to justice the tort-feasor, who surely has no moral or any other right to rely on decisions of the appellate courts?

As an abstract matter, there surely was no justice in the age-old doctrine denying a recovery to a child for prenatal injuries. When that was overruled and *stare decisis* fell, was there anything unjust? Could anyone justly contend that he could rely on injuring pregnant women with impunity because, as a matter of *stare decisis*, that was the law?

When these ghosts of the past such as *stare decisis* stand in the path of justice, clanking their medieval chains, an English judge is reported to have said, the court must follow a course only to pass them undeterred.

It is sometimes difficult to perceive the rationale of affirmances in civil cases. Take a case that has been to the appellate court twice and on each occasion has been turned back as against justice, as against the weight of credible evidence, or as the product of the obvious bias and prejudice of the fact finders. Yet on the very next occasion, for the same case and on the same facts, though abstract justice may demand adherence to the same view, a mechanical surrender may affirm what has been found unpalatable.

Is it enough to say that there must be an end of civil appeals if that end is an unjust end?

Perplexing and difficult cases are continually appearing in which the narrowest margin separates the rights of the respective parties. The matter may lie so evenly and the appropriate legal rule to be applied may be so doubtful that the keenest and most vigorous mind finds difficulty in determining on which side of the scales of justice and equity the legal result should lie.

In these cases it is not unlikely that the judges on appeal can easily persuade themselves that justice requires that decision which best accords with their own background, social philosophy, feelings, and ulterior views. The extraordinary thing in these cases is that members of the court, drawn from diverse backgrounds and of varied training, will so frequently arrive at the very same result. Abstract justice, therefore, is no sure guide to the result of a civil appeal.

One suggested approach to civil appeals is to create a constructive dialogue between scholars whenever complicated states of fact arise. Is there any reason why in complicated cases appellate courts should not request the disinterested opinions of scholars as *amici curiae* so that all will have the benefit of their views and an opportunity to present questions to them?

Consider, if you will, the advances in the arts and sciences, such as modern electronics, computerization, chemistry, physics, and many others. It cannot be assumed with any assurance that our modern jurists have come equipped to grapple with such matters on the basis of past technical knowledge and experience. Indeed, it has become a major challenge in a complicated appeal when the matter turns heavily on an appreciation of technical subjects to present the case adequately for review by nonspecialists.

In a comparison of law and scientific method, Prof. Morris R. Cohen wrote many, many years ago:

> We find appellate courts making all sorts of factual generalizations without adequate information. The facilities of our courts for acquiring information as to the actual conditions are very limited. Courts have to decide all sorts of complicated issues after only a few hours of oral argument and briefs by lawyers.

Now to another subject. We frequently meet what may be described as intuitive generalizations from the bench on civil appeals. True it is that many legal discussions in the area of civil cases, for example, those in the law of real property, are very largely devoid of any moral or social ideals. They rest entirely on the application of legal rules. There is, therefore, no intuitive generalization to which resort can be made or with which we need be concerned.

Llewellyn, in analyzing the habits of judicial thought, expressed his view as follows:

> The common process in reaching decisions is in a measure one of sudden intuition, a leap to some result that eases the tension for the judge, or else it is a process of successive mental experiments as imagination develops and

passes in review various possibilities until one or more turns up which has appeal. In any ordinary case, a reasoned justification for the result represents the subsequent job.

To meet these intuitive reactions, it becomes the task of the appellate advocate on civil appeals to anticipate and guide the judge largely by presenting the lessons of experience. He must present the competing propositions that are likely to form the basis from which the decision will emerge.

The common feature to be found in the relevant cases must be abstracted by the advocate and a general principle or concept thereon submitted. Analogies or examples become various and very frequently are adopted and appear in the opinions. Making judging easy is a device for bringing the appeal to the conclusion sought by the advocate.

Of course, a major problem that is possibly insoluble is how to determine what will trouble or interest the court. Plainly, selecting the argument to be made is a form of addressing the court on a subject of its interest and concern.

I wonder whether we are not overlooking some important means of improving the appellate process as we know it today. The ideal posture for an appeal would be one in which there was agreement among counsel and the court on the choice and ranking of the issues and on the material lines of reasoning on those issues. For convenience, let's call this the consensus.

The skilled appellate counsel's art lies in trying to persuade the appellate judges that his choice and ranking of the issues in the order of importance are the proper choice and ranking, that his lines of reasoning on the issues are the proper lines. The advocate's art, of course, lies in posturing the case, in dominating the appeal while at the same time he tries to meet all the appellant's arguments.

I might add at this point that probably the single greatest difficulty in structuring the appellee's brief is to find the right balance in a particular case between joining issue head on with the appellant, on the one hand, and formulating the issues as the appellee sees them, on the other, with rebuttal only a secondary aspect of his preparation. Appellees' briefs overstress rebuttal as often as they overstress the restructuring of the issues.

In the middle of all this, of course, are the judges. Ultimately their own conception of the choice and ranking of the issues and of the most fruitful lines of reasoning will determine the case.

Appellate judges are only a vague image in the mind of counsel preparing for combat on appeal. The reason is simply that until oral argument the judge has not assumed any place in the preparation of the appeal.

At the oral argument, he may or may not give counsel some idea of his ranking of the issues and of his notion of materiality of the lines of argument. But it may then be too late for the judge's probing to be really productive. If the judge has not read the briefs before oral argument, he runs the risk of his own quickness and accuracy in seeing the case whole at that time. He runs the further risk that counsel will be unprepared to help him if his view of important points and lines of reasoning is different from theirs.

Even if the judge has read the briefs before argument, he runs the risk of counsel's unpreparedness or confusion. Then, too, any lawyer who really believes that he will win if the judge truly understands the case is running an equal risk. Many judges prefer to postpone the reading of briefs until after argument. Perhaps if judges could be promised less work and time between briefing and opinion, there would be a wider application of the practice in some courts of reading briefs before argument.

This is precisely what the notion of a consensus would achieve. Judges, too, would prepare for argument and briefing. Argument, decision, and opinion writing would be considerably sharpened and shortened.

How then should we attempt to achieve this concensus? We shall never do it perfectly, but we could take a step forward by adding a third stage to the brief writing, one that brings the judges into active participation. The primary stage as we know it now is the main brief. The secondary stage is the reply. The third stage might be the framing of written questions by the appellate judges before oral argument and the forwarding of documental answers as the last stage of briefing.

Of course, I would never eliminate utter freedom of counsel and the appellate bench to make and hear oral argument, ask questions from the bench, and structure the case finally in the living context of spontaneous dialogue.

The present method is for the parties to depart after the argument and for the judge to have his clerk look up the law, wrestle with the matters that trouble the judge, and then supply a memorandum for his guidance. But this discards the two most knowledgeable sources on the case, the lawyers who probably have spent weeks and weeks on facts, law, and perspective of the issues.

The Supreme Court of the United States utilizes two

techniques for sharpening the focus of the questions brought before it. Sometimes it grants certiorari limited to a specific question. Another technique is to direct the attention of the parties to the question that interests the Court, as in a recent case in which the Court, in granting a writ of certiorari to the United States Court of Appeals for the Sixth Circuit, requested the parties to brief and argue the question of the retroactivity of the doctrine announced in *Griffin v California*.

The New Jersey Supreme Court, as I understand it, has a conference before it hears an appeal and chooses the point in the appeal it wishes to have developed. One writer on New Jersey practice says:

> Under the present system, each justice has had an opportunity to study the record and the briefs before the argument and frequently the court will request counsel to limit his argument to a specific question.

One immediately apparent disadvantage of the New Jersey system is that counsel may not know what the court is primarily interested in until he gets up to make his oral argument. The point may be some aspect of the case to which he perhaps has intended to devote very little of his presentation.

Our own Appellate Division of the First Department adopted an interesting and, I believe, unusual approach in a recent case concerning the World Trade Center. After it had heard oral argument, the court apparently concluded either that certain aspects of the case had not been fully treated in the briefs or that the progress of the appeal had developed problems which had not been foreseen. At any rate, a week later it published in the *Law Journal* a request that counsel submit supplemental briefs in which they would set forth their answers to four specific questions. The parties did so, and the appeal was decided in due course.

Undoubtedly an appellate court in quest of justice can do, and often has done, more reformulating of badly drawn issues than is generally realized even by lawyers. But how often does the court that sets out to reformulate the issues give counsel an opportunity to submit new briefs?

There are, of course, instances on appeals when counsel on both sides are agreed that the question which may ultimately trouble the court has nothing to do with the case. Under the present system of appeals in our state, the parties remain unheard on the question when the case is finally submitted and the court must then wrestle with the matter without counsel's aid.

It is also true that appellate judges sometimes take over and decide the issue that they want to decide rather than the case presented by the parties. A startling example was the case of *Erie v Tompkins*, which overruled *Swift v Tyson*. The decided issue was not at all what had been postured in the District Court or in the Court of Appeals.

Indeed, it is sometimes suspected that an appellate judge has a canned documented opinion or viewpoint which he has worked up on the subject of his particular interests and is waiting for a case in which he can supply the work even if it means straining the perimeter of the issues actually presented for decision. While that may be stating the matter a little too broadly, this conceivably could have happened in the *Palsgraf* case against the Long Island Rail Road.

As the story goes, Judge Cardozo sat in on a session at the American Law Institute when the problem of whether liability should go beyond the orbit of risk was being debated. The lady in the case apparently was hit on the head by a scale that knocked her over because there was an explosion at the other end of the station. In the normal course of events, she was protected under a rule that the railroad owed her a duty of care. While the case was in the Appellate Division and before it ever got to the Court of Appeals, the American Law Institute debated and debated the issue of whether there should be a limitation to the orbit of risk. And that's the decision that ultimately was made in the Court of Appeals, 4 to 3. Judge Cardozo sat in on the sessions, and although he didn't participate, it is quite obvious that he was aware of the debates when the case reached the Court of Appeals.

The question is sometimes asked: How should a case be handled that looks as though it is an extension of principle, an extension of liability? Basically, I would say that the conservative approach, not letting on to the court that the court is breaking new ground, is the safest. Judges basically are conservative and not lawmakers, they say.

When intense prejudice or controversy has operated against the appellant, need he be fully vindicated? Some years ago, in a case that has now become part of a best seller, the individual involved seemed to have an excellent legal position, but his position in society was not as good as that which he had in the case. The advocate believed that a personal vindication of his client was unnecessary and probably unattainable and that he didn't have to make this client smell like a rose to obtain a favorable legal result. In such a situation, the technique was to endeavor to dispel the notion that the advocate was trying to raise the client in the court's estimation.

Of course it happened that all this was to no avail. The presiding judge pierced the device by intoning that the evidence would not carry the theory argued, and in a few short weeks the controversy qualified by judicial decision for a place in a leading best seller.

The *Duane Jones* case is an interesting one to consider. One might ask why the case did not get a better result in the Appellate Division than 3 to 2. The Appellate Division affirmed the decision of the jury. It is true that the court moved the case to higher ground. The plaintiff's approach in the Appellate Division was to endeavor to satisfy the court that nothing unusual had been decided, that what had been found to be a breach of faith and fiduciary principle was the kind of thing that happened on Seventh Avenue all the time, every day. Counsel argued that the only difference in this case was that the hand that reached into the cash register got jammed on the way out for all to see and that the nine who were cast in judgment had done the awful thing of competing from within the premises before they left for their own occupations.

The reason why it was assumed that the case moved to higher ground lay in the defendants' argument that the rule of law holding these employees to a liability would set off a round of explosions in all the professions. They posited the case, if my memory serves me correctly, of the lawyer in a large law firm who services clients and then leaves the firm and finds himself endowed with the business of those clients. Would that not provoke a claim on the part of the law firm to recapture the business?

The appellants' approach was that Duane Jones, in effect, was losing this business anyhow; he was allegedly addicted to an unfortunate habit; and, under the circumstances, the men were entitled to salvage their own lives. With that kind of approach, it became necessary to deal with the matter head on. The simple illustration of the drunk in the subway who couldn't be rolled merely because he was drunk seemed to capture more interest than the notion that this poor laboring crowd was going to be deprived of an opportunity of free enterprise. The appellee's approach was to emphasize the equities, fiduciary standards, trust obligations, dismembering a victim.

The court's reaction in the Appellate Division, 3 to 2, was that disparagement and personalities lost out to trust obligation; that knowing participation in the events and absent personal profit from the conspiracy won 3 to 2 over the conspirators, jointly liable.

It is clear that the majority opinion in the Appellate Division reflected the arguments of counsel, and when the case finally got to the Court of Appeals, the issue turned very largely on the policy question whether, in a situation that was ambiguous, trust obligation would be the means of determining how the conduct of the party should be judged.

In summary, the approach on the civil appeal is to look over the case, determine where the equities are, look over the judges, determine whether they are prepared for you and you are prepared for them, and learn whether they are going to be listeners, be aggressive, or be quizzical.

Organize your script and paint the picture with simplicity and brevity, alertness and sensitivity, particularly to the chance remark from the bench that may be a smoke signal for you. Align yourself, if you can, with the opinion to be written—what would *you* say if you had to write the opinion. Point up the crucial issue and involve the judge on your side. Shift him to the role of an advocate for you.

Every man's method will vary on a civil appeal, but all methods are designed to achieve the same end, namely, to present prejudicial error on material matters or, as the appellee, to establish that such error is absent. It is too much for anyone to hope for a measure of success beyond the averages recorded for appellate results. That brings me to the end of this opportunity to give you my views on some aspects of the civil appeal.

QUESTION PERIOD

QUESTION: You have advised that we make sure the court considers the issues in the ranking that we prefer because most of the cases will be decided on the basis of how the issues are ranked. Now, if you have judges trying to rerank you out of your line of issues, how do you bring them back?

MR. POLLACK: The only way to bring them back is to get them into an argument. If you are unable to provoke controversy in the appellate courtroom, you are going to find that the judges will go off to their chambers browsing in the direction in which they want to browse, and in your particular case you will be unheard.

If the judge begins to rustle his papers and indicates no interest in what you are doing or saying, say something provocative—anything—that will capture his attention. Insult him if you have to, call him by name, point out some previous experience, but get him into a conversation. It is the interchange of conversation with the judge that will enable you to lead him skillfully and carefully into the range of thinking what you want. This is your only chance to convince him before he gets into conference.

QUESTION: Would you retain other counsel to argue an appeal when the counsel who tried the case in the court below is able, knows the situation, has gone over the testimony, and has been there but feels that his client should get the best treatment before the appellate court?

MR. POLLACK: The best man to argue a case is the man who has been through the birth pains of the case. If he knows the record and has the feel of the case and if he has the conscience to do the job for the client, he is better than any Hessian you can import.

The question that you face is: Is he organized mentally to prepare a plan of attack within a very confined, short period of time to carry the message to the court? Some people are gifted in that way; others are gifted at the trial level. Very few combine the two qualities.

Rarely is it necessary, in my judgment, for someone who is versed in the case and who has the feel for the client and his cause to import anybody from the outside. He ought to take a chance and present the case himself.

QUESTION: My question has to do with the matter of judgment. Let's assume you are up arguing an appeal and, by questioning between the court and yourself, you feel that you are ahead of the game and that the judges are coming along with you. Do you continue for the full length of your argument, or do you quit when you think you are ahead?

MR. POLLACK: It is very dangerous to assume that you can read correctly what you hear in the courtroom. Very frequently a judge will attempt to be helpful to a particular side by bringing out the matters that he thinks one of his colleagues may raise in the conference. He becomes a sort of interlocutor. It is a mistake to believe that he is necessarily on your side. All that he is doing, perhaps, is informing himself or informing his colleagues.

Unless you have carried the point that you are prepared to carry to the court, reliance on the smoke signals and signals from the bench may only mean that you have relied on one judge out of the five or one out of the seven, and that doesn't help you win. You need three or four.

QUESTION: I would like to ask Dr. Pollack about his advice regarding selectivity, since as he stated and as I agree, an appellate court will frequently decide a case on a point deemed unimportant by counsel. How can the principle of selectivity be applied when you see error? How can you make up your mind that a point is not significant enough to be briefed? Should you not include it in your brief? Are you not acting as the judge in your own case, which you said the appellate lawyer should not do, in leaving the point out of the brief?

MR. POLLACK: An expert doesn't make mistakes in selectivity. You don't prove a case by proving every point in the case. I think you do prove the case by leading the court in the direction in which you want to lead it. But when you have proved the case right down to the last degree, it becomes suspect.

I think that the same thing is true of jury appeals. When a lawyer argues a case to a jury, he doesn't argue every inch of the evidence. He creates the aura of the case, gives some excellent illustrations and some corroborative facts, and lets the jury find the balance. I think that that is the technique to follow on appeal. Let the judges have the credit of having found your remaining points. Pick the ones that are sure winners and let the judges find the others.

QUESTION: Assume that you have represented a plaintiff who has been very successful below and that the jury has been most generous to him. You come to the appellate argument, and you get the impression from the court that the verdict is going down a little bit. You get the invariable question: "What do you think your plaintiff should get?" How do you field that question?

MR. POLLACK: "Everything that he got. I am not sure that the jury appraised the full extent of the injury. It seems to me that they could have given a full verdict, but I am satisfied with their compromise." Perhaps Judge Breitel would like to comment.

JUDGE BREITEL: It is a very difficult question, and I personally never ask it; I don't see any point to it. I think it forces the lawyer pretty much into a situation in which he has virtually to offer settlement on the appellate argument as if the appeal were a pretrial. The question can be embarrassing. It has happened that the lawyer has given a figure lower than the one that he was most likely to get from the court. Then the figure that he used was repeated in conference to his disadvantage.

I would try to avoid an answer one way or the other. I suppose, one could simply say it is not your province at this point to give a figure. It is your job to point out the pluses and the minuses and let it go at that.

References Made by Mr. Pollack

CASES

Griffin v California (1965) 380 US 609

Duane Jones Co. v Burke (1953) 281 App Div 622, 121 NYS2d 107, mod, 306 NY 172, 117 NE2d 237

Erie *v* Tompkins (1938) 304 US 64
Palsgraf *v* Long Island R. Co. (1927) 225 NYS 412, *rev'd* 248 NY
   339, 162 NE 99
Swift *v* Tyson (1842) 41 US (16 Pet) 1

OTHER

Nizer, Louis, *My Life in Court*, Doubleday, Garden City, N.Y., 1961.

The Civil and the Criminal
Appeal Compared

WHITMAN KNAPP

Whitman Knapp, a member of The Association of
the Bar of the City of New York and the New York
County, New York State, and American Bar
Associations, received his legal education at the
Harvard Law School. He spent eight years as an
assistant district attorney for New York County and
is currently a partner in the firm of Knapp,
Barrett, Smith and Schapiro in New York City.
A member of the American Law Institute and the
American College of Trial Lawyers, he has had
extensive experience in the litigation of
both civil and criminal matters.

Before I start, I want to put your minds at ease about the pamphlet that has been distributed.[1] In the first place, I don't intend to talk about all these cases or even about most of them. Since the pamphlet was printed, you will all be greatly relieved to hear, I have done a great deal of pruning.

The cases are set forth in three categories, criminal appeals, civil appeals, and legislative appeals. Now you may wonder what the term "legislative appeals" means and why it is there. It is there for a very good purpose. It is there to make you stay to the end to find out what it means.

We shall start off with the civil and criminal appeals. I am supposed to compare the two. Presumably, therefore, I am supposed to tell you why they are different.

The first thing you notice about civil and criminal cases is that superficially, at least, they are exactly the same. They have basically the same rules of evidence, although the rules are a little bit easier in criminal cases, as I shall show you; the same rules of trial procedure; and the same, or basically similar, formal rules of appeal—how you write your brief, what your brief has to contain, the order of presentation of argument, etc.

However, within the area of our discussion this evening —effective advocacy before a court—I shall submit to you that the two are entirely different; that the rules that apply to one are absolutely the opposite of those for the other.

[1] See p. 99.

In the civil appeal, your basic objective as an appellate advocate should be to convince the court that, as between the parties, the substantive result below was fundamentally wrong and that the error was not attributable to your client or to your predecessor. And, if at all possible, you should convince the court that the legal position you are asking it to take will permit it either to provide for or to set the stage for a final disposition of the controversy.

Of course, you can't make this approach in every civil case, and to the extent that any one of these basic arguments is unavailable in any given case, you have special problems that I hope we shall come to later on this evening.

To recapitulate, I don't think I shall get much argument or dissent from you when I say your basic objective in a civil case is to convince the court that there is a fundamental wrongness (I don't like to use the word "injustice," because that gets me into all kinds of arguments over what it means) in the result below and that the court can, by adopting your argument, see some end to the litigation and not be opening a Pandora's box of interminable proceedings between the parties.

As I have indicated, I don't expect much disagreement on that point. But I do expect some dissent to the proposition that I shall now make to you with respect to the criminal appeal, namely, that the considerations are exactly the opposite. It is my submission that, as an appellant in a criminal case, you should avoid like the plague any attempt to get the court involved in the question of whether substantial justice was done between your client and the government.

Whatever individual judges may think of their attitude

on this subject, and I have had some arguments about the point with our chairman, I am convinced that to a man they have a fundamental reluctance to get involved in that question and will resent and resist you all the way if you attempt to involve them in it.

Your objective then, I submit to you, should be to avoid any concern for ultimate justice as between the parties and, so far as possible, such matters as the sufficiency of the evidence, and to convince the court that there was some basic procedural irregularity in the process that resulted in the conviction. It doesn't make much difference whether that irregularity was in the prearrest process, in the grand jury proceedings, or at any point up to and including the verdict.

It doesn't make a bit of difference whether some form of stupidity on the part of your client or your own produced the irregularity that you are complaining about. It is, however, of the utmost importance that the proposition you are urging will not bring an end to the case, will not forever foreclose the prosecution from another chance at conviction. All you want to do is to let your client live to fight another day.

The basic distinction, then, that I suggest between the civil and the criminal appeal is this: in the one, the court wants to get to the final issue and achieve a final result; in the other, the court shies from involvement in the substantive result and wants anything but finality.

Why the difference? Well, to understand the criminal appeal or at least my theories about it, you must first understand my theories about the entire criminal process; so let's take a look at them.

Criminal law is a nasty and archaic business: taking a

man from his home, locking him up, or even killing him. It's an uncivilized business, and whether we admit it or not, we are all basically ashamed of it. Don't get the idea that I think I have a better way of dealing with the problem of crime. Neither I nor, so far as I know, anyone else has come up with a better solution. Nonetheless, it is a messy business, and we are all ashamed of it.

We have gotten more civilized or more squeamish in the recent centuries, and no one wants to take responsibility for killing a man or for locking him up. It isn't as it was in the days of the first efforts at smoke control, when, as I read in a recent editorial in the *New York Times*, King Henry I came upon an ironmonger who was making too much smoke. He read him a lecture and had him hanged on the spot.

So what have we done to protect law-enforcement officials—and they include the police, the prosecutor, the jurors, and the trial and appellate judges—from getting so mixed up in the mess that, being civilized human beings, they are unable to function? We have devised a complicated system, operating under well-defined rules, whereby no individual human being is required to take total responsibility for anything but whereby every individual can concentrate on his or her small task and leave ultimate responsibility up in the air. The police investigate. The prosecutor prepares and presents his case. The judge lays down the rules. The jurors, each sharing his responsibility with eleven others, make the finding of fact. The trial judge, with a complicated and formal statutory system and a detailed probation report to fall back on, imposes sentence. Finally the appellate court, from its Olympian heights, reviews the situation and makes sure that everyone has played the game according to the rules.

The essential lubricating agent that makes this process possible is the ability of each person in the chain to have confidence in the essential competence and integrity of every other such person. If the district attorney had no confidence in the police, he couldn't long run his office. If the trial court and the jurors had no confidence in the prosecutor, there would be no conviction. If the appellate judges didn't have essential confidence in the integrity and competence (basically, the integrity) of the prosecutor and of the entire judicial system over which they preside and felt that they had to examine the justice of every case before them, they would soon find themselves so overwhelmed that they could not carry out their functions.

The point is this: the appellate judges know that they must function and that the system must survive. They, therefore, have a strong vested interest in their belief in the integrity of the system, the belief that affords them the necessary isolation from individual responsibility.

It follows that if you come to them with a contention that the system has totally failed, that the jury's finding is so wrong as to require them to assume responsibility for reappraising it, the appellate judges are going to resent your argument and set their minds against agreeing with anything you have to say. In short, it is my oversimplified suggestion that no appellant's brief should ever have a point that "guilt was not established beyond a reasonable doubt."

Perhaps I can illustrate my philosophy of the criminal law in general and of appeals in particular by discussing in some depth a case with which I was intimately concerned back in 1947 when I was in the District Attorney's office, *People v John Dunn*, one of those listed in the pamphlet with which you have been provided. That case illustrates several of my theories about the criminal law and about criminal appeals. First, it illustrates my theory that it takes less evidence to establish a given fact in a criminal case than it would to establish the same fact in a civil trial. Second, it gives dramatic support to my theory of divided responsibility. Finally, it provides a nice laboratory specimen with which, with all the freedom of a medical examiner doing an autopsy, we can speculate concerning my theories about the criminal appeal.

Now the basic facts in that case were simple and gruesome. One Andy Hintz was a longshore labor official who had the trait of being honest. That trait, a most peculiar one back in 1947, got him in trouble with one John Dunn, a notorious labor racketeer. One January morning as Andy Hintz started out to work, he met John Dunn and two henchmen in the hallway of the tenement where he lived. They pumped five .38-caliber bullets into his body and left him lying on the stairway. About two hours later, the police found John Dunn sipping coffee in his office.

Now I mentioned John Dunn and two henchmen. For simplicity, I shall refer to only one of the henchmen. From now on, I shall talk about only two persons. A different consideration applied to the third, to whom I shall not refer.

This would have been like any other unsolved gangland killing, except that Andy Hintz had the ill grace to linger for twenty days. He was supposed to have died on the spot. During this time he made some five statements or declarations about the shooting. Three of these, made at the moments when Andy thought he was dying, inculpated one or more of the defendants. The last two inculpated all. The other two statements, made at a time when Andy seemed to be getting better and hoped to live, completely exonerated all the defendants. It was quite clear that Andy Hintz had decided that if he ever got well, he wanted to stay that way.

Aside from these declarations, there was, as to the defendant Dunn, no evidence whatever except for some so-called admissions to one Tough Tony Tischon, a fellow inmate in the Tombs who was awaiting trial. Anyone who knows anything about criminal law knows that such prison admissions are highly suspect. Prisoners, especially those awaiting sentence, show extreme ingenuity in dreaming up testimony that they believe will be helpful and that they can sell as valid even to the most alert prosecutor.

As to Dunn, we have just these dying declarations and so-called admissions. As to the second defendant, there was absolutely no evidence connecting him with the killing except for the dying declarations.

Now the law of New York is that a dying declaration, that is to say, a declaration made by a person who is *in extremis*, who has given up all hope of recovery and actually does die of the condition from which he is suffering, is admissible in evidence in a prosecution for homicide against the person charged with being responsible for the declarant's condition. However, there had at that time never been a decision in New York as to whether a dying declaration would, without more, support a judgment of conviction. The two times the question had been presented to the Court of Appeals, in *Bartelini* and *Ludkowitz*, two of the other cases listed in the pamphlet, the court had ducked the question, ruled that the dying declarations were admissible, pointed out how dangerous they were, and ordered a new trial on grounds of technical error.

Those are the facts and the law. What does the case show about the three theories I have mentioned?

Well, as to the first theory, the difference between civil and criminal cases, the point is rather easy. Dying declarations aren't even admissible in civil cases. Therefore, if this had been a civil action for wrongful death by the widow, the case would never have gotten off the ground. Moreover, even if dying declarations were admissible in civil cases (as they are in Kansas, Arkansas, and Colorado), I doubt whether the widow's action, stripped of all the drama of a criminal trial, would ever have gotten to first base.

What about the division of responsibility? Well, the police's job was simple. They were faced with an accusation of vicious assault and later of murder, and all they had to do was find the accused, arrest them, and help the prosecutor build his case.

The prosecutor's responsibility was more complex. He had to decide whether these dying declarations were to be trusted and whether, morally as well as legally, they warranted the death penalty for the persons accused.

The preliminary responsibility fell to George Monaghan, in charge of Homicide. He decided the case should be dismissed because in his view, as a matter of law, no conviction that might be obtained could be sustained on appeal.

The district attorney, Frank Hogan, declined to approve until I, who was in charge of appeals, should concur. I, after careful consideration of *Bartelini* and *Ludkowitz*, said that it could not be said that the evidence was insufficient as a matter of law. I thought it highly likely that the Court of Appeals would, as it had done in *Bartelini* and *Ludkowitz*, seize upon any error to reverse, and I thought it quite unlikely that George would be able to get a verdict, let alone one wholly untainted with legal error. But I could not say that there was no case as a matter of law.

And so the decision was made. Mr. Hogan had the integrity of his office to maintain, which he did. I was responsible for a legal opinion, which I gave. To Monaghan fell the task of convincing the jury.

Now I by no means wish to suggest that any of us had personal doubt of the defendants' guilt. But there is a whale of a difference between not having personal doubt about something someone else must ultimately decide and being prepared to take sole responsibility for an individual's imprisonment or even death.

Well, the trial was a bitter one. It lasted about four weeks, but justice ultimately prevailed. That is, all defendants were convicted. The jury, however, took about thirty hours of uninterrupted deliberations before reaching this verdict. So now we come to the appeal.

I guess it won't surprise you when I say that during this four-week trial many things happened that caused me gravely to doubt that the Court of Appeals would deem this record to present that pristine purity it had specified, in *Bartelini* and *Ludkowitz*, as prerequisite to the validity of a conviction predicated exclusively on a dying declaration. I, personally, was most seriously troubled by a vicious campaign of newspaper publicity that had been carried on, principally by the now-defunct *Daily Mirror*. The purpose of this campaign, which went on during the whole trial, was to convince *Mirror* readers that Dunn was a vicious gangster who must surely be convicted unless Hogan's office was incompetent or worse.

I, for one, was never satisfied that the jurors, despite their pious denials every time they were asked by the judge, had not been influenced by this vicious campaign. They had been instructed by the judge not to read the papers, and they duly said they hadn't read them. However, most of the publicity was in the form of front-page editorials, gruesomely illustrated, and I never could understand how the jurors could have gotten to and from their homes without becoming aware of, and being in some measure influenced by, the paper's campaign. As some of you may remember, the hotel situation in 1947 made it impracticable to lock up a jury during trial.

Faced with this situation, what did appellants' counsel do? What do I, as guide to you in this postmortem, think they should have done?

Taking the latter question first, it is my submission that, despite (and even because of) the very close question that had been before the jury, which it took thirty hours of continuous deliberations to resolve, the appellants should have made no attack on the sufficiency of the evidence. On the contrary, both in the brief and in oral argument, they should, I submit, simply have stated the evidence completely and accurately as to all essentials but in a succinct and uninteresting style slanted to emphasize the unassailable proposition that the dying declaration provided the only real evidence connecting these defendants with the crime.

They should then have specifically conceded that the court in *Ludkowitz* and *Bartelini* had refused to declare such evidence insufficient. But in the same breath they should have confronted the court with its own language in those cases, which language graphically expressed the great mistrust with which the court regarded such evidence and the extreme care it felt was necessary to be certain that any verdict based thereon was wholly untainted by any improper consideration.

With the stage thus set, the appellants, I submit to you, should have embarrassed the court with these newspaper articles about which I have been speaking and should have referred to whatever other errors seemed pertinent, especially errors that were tied to the newspaper publicity. For example, in the heat of his argument, George Monaghan had several times referred to an "underworld code." Well, there is nothing in the record about an underworld code. But anyone who had read the *Mirror* would have had no doubt as to what he was talking about.

With the groundwork thus laid, the appellants should then have squarely put to the court the question whether it could, in good conscience, say that the rigid requirements of *Ludkowitz* and *Bartelini* had been met.

In other words, starting off with the court's declared distrust of dying declarations in general, the appellants should have tried to particularize that distrust by undermining the court's confidence in the conditions under which these particular dying declarations had been considered by the jury. They should not have attacked the prosecution in any way. Indeed, they should have sympathized with it in its duty in presenting this case and then in effect have said to the court: "Let us reason together and see whether or not this particular case is that rare situation you envisioned in *Ludkowitz* and *Bartelini* in which it would be proper to send a defendant to his death on no more evidence than a dying declaration." The appellants should have avoided like the plague any discussion of the declarations themselves or of the actions of the defendants that those declarations depicted.

What in fact was done? Well, while the attorneys did argue one or more of the errors, the bulk of their briefs was devoted to attacking the verdict on its merits. Take, for example, the oral argument. For about two hours the great advocates who represented these defendants hammered home before the court the inadequacy of the evidence. What were they actually doing? They were telling the court in effect, though not in words, that Frank Hogan had acted irresponsibly in bringing the case to trial, that Judge Donellan had acted irresponsibly in submitting it to the jury, and, of course, that the jury had acted irresponsibly in its verdict. Now, those were propositions that the judges were bound to resist and resent, and as I rose to make my argument, I could almost feel them pleading with me to supply adequate answers to these disturbing accusations—an assignment I was most happy to undertake.

My argument, and it lasted an hour and a half, as I remember it, was devoted exclusively to fact, blood, and death: the drama of the killing, of Andy Hintz's first declaration to his wife as she swabbed the blood from his face, of his twenty-day fight for life, with the ebb and flow, on the one hand, of his fear of the defendants and consequent denials of his accusations when he thought he was recovering and, on the other hand, of his desire for vengeance and consequent reassertion of his accusations as he thought he was facing death. I hardly mentioned the trial throughout my argument. I talked only about declarations and about death.

To give you an idea of the tone of the argument, let me read to you a few of the opening sentences in the statement of the evidence contained in my brief. It starts out:

> Evidence, People's case, killing.
> At about seven-forty A.M. on January 8th, 1947, at the door of their third floor apartment at 61 Grove Street, Daisy Hintz kissed her husband good-bye as he left for work. A few moments later she heard what she thought was backfire. Then four or five shots. Her husband's voice cried out something which she missed, and then, "Dunn, Dunn." Rushing out in horror she saw her husband lying on the landing below, face down. A neighbor, Mrs. Margaret Tarlan, testified that within a minute or forty-five seconds after the shots she heard a man cry, "Daisy, Daisy." A woman replied, "I am coming, I am coming, who shot you?"
> And the man said, "Johnny did it."

And so went the rest of the brief or, rather, the rest of the statement of facts. As to the questions of law, as I already indicated, none was even mentioned on the oral argument.

On the brief, my associates and I devised an entirely new brief form. So far as I know, it had never been used before and has never been used again. Each question raised or suggested by the defendants was treated in a single paragraph with absolute accuracy and insufferable dullness.

Now what was the total impact of this attack by the defendants and response by the People? It got the court, against its own inclinations, totally involved in the question of the defendants' guilt or innocence, a question that it was predisposed to answer in the People's favor. After all, Frank Hogan does not and did not have a reputation for making irresponsible accusations. The result was that all questions about newspaper publicity and other claims of error dropped out of sight.

We can only speculate whether a different approach would have brought about a different result. I can only suggest that a more hopeful approach from the appellants' point of view would have been one that did not make a head-on attack on the People's case. It certainly would have prevented me from making the kind of response that I felt was the only one which could possibly have won that case.

Enough of speculation. Let us turn to a case in which the appeal was actually conducted in accordance with my theory. However, I want to make clear that, so far as I know, the appellant's lawyer in this case had never heard either of me or of my theories at the time he made the argument in question.

The case to which I refer is *People v Richardson*, the opinion of which is set forth in full in the pamphlet before you.[1] The case illustrates not only the propositions we are here discussing but, as I shall demonstrate, the truth that you should never ask a judge how to argue an appeal.

The facts in this case are relatively simple. One Chong, a Chinese waiter who lived on the tenth floor of a building in the Alfred E. Smith development, was robbed by three men as he left the apartment-house elevator when it reached his floor. His assailants had gone up in the elevator with him. When questioned by the police, however, Chong could give only a vague description of his assailants and said he would not be able to recognize them if he saw them again.

However, the police found three men lurking in the neighborhood, and when Chong was confronted with these suspects, he identified them as his assailants. There was some mildly corroborative evidence, including a conversation between the defendants and the police officer just before arraignment, which conversation might, possibly, have been construed as an admission that the three men had been together just before the robbery, a position contrary to the one that they took at trial.

Now there was a pretty weak case. One might wonder how the People ever got a conviction. Indeed, returning to our chairman's opening remarks about the relative difficulties of getting verdicts in criminal and civil cases, I rather suspect that had Mr. Chong brought a civil action for assault, he wouldn't have gotten a verdict. I rather think the jury might have taken him at his word when he said he wouldn't be able to identify the people if he saw them.

However, the defendant's lawyer on appeal—and the

[1] See page 101.

reason I know about this is that I was there waiting for a case of my own to be argued—flatly disavowed any attack on the sufficiency of the evidence. Instead, he spent practically his whole argument and, I presume, his brief in talking about the defendant's prearraignment quasi-admission, the conversation they had just before arraignment, and in demonstrating that as constitutional law is now developing, this admission should not have been allowed in evidence. As you can see from the opinion, the court bought that argument. In passing, the court also accepted counsel's criticism of the People's order of proof.

Now this business of not attacking the sufficiency of the evidence did not sit too well with all the judges. Indeed, one of them, who shall be nameless but who sits quite near where I am now standing, interrupted counsel several times and criticized his failure to make a point of sufficiency. But arguing counsel stuck to his position and simply replied that he did not think such a point would be valid. And that dramatically illustrates our chairman's original observation that you should not ask a judge how to argue an appeal.

I put it to you that had the appellant challenged the sufficiency of the evidence, he would have lost the appeal. The judges would then have gotten involved in that problem and would have concluded, as in fact they did, that the evidence presented a fair jury question. You will note that nothing in the opinion sending the case back for a new trial suggests that more evidence would be needed to support a conviction. Consequently, it is my submission that if counsel had got the court involved in the question of guilt, the judges would have been put in a frame of mind to regard as quite inconsequential his finely spun argument on constitutional law governing this really unimportant conversation.

The point is that judges decide a case only once; and judges are human beings, and judges are advocates. If you get a judge riled on an advocate's point against you, it's unrealistic to assume that he will reverse his field and decide some minor point in your favor. I don't believe any such thing would have happened in this case.

As I conclude this phase of my subject, don't let me leave you with the impression that you should ignore the evidence. That may be fatal because the court may think that you are afraid of it. What you must do is state the evidence succinctly and briefly but sufficiently completely so that the People's brief can't produce any surprises. State it in such a way as to show that a real jury question exists, and then hammer some point which will rob the court of its ability to say with confidence that the jury was wholly uninfluenced by any breach of the rules of the game.

In talking about statements of evidence, perhaps I can devote a minute to a case I once handled. I've just said that you should make statements of evidence so complete as to leave no surprises for the People to produce. Well, that's not universally true either, if you have a reason for wanting the People to surprise the court. In the case I mentioned, it was my point that there had been too many lawyers so frequently changed as to make adequate preparation for trial impossible. My total reference to the evidence follows:

> The deceased was a white man who apparently had gone into a Harlem hallway and had met his death resisting a

robbery. Defendant was arrested eight days after the event. The only witnesses purporting to link him with the killing were two prostitutes, each of whom was a mainliner heroin addict. It is our contention that the defendant, in effect, had no lawyer and was not accorded a legal trial.

Now that was not all the evidence there was in the case. A whale of a lot of evidence of incriminating circumstances got into the case through the defense. They put on alibi witnesses who quite obviously lied, and they put on the defendant himself, and after listening to his testimony, you concluded that if he didn't kill this particular man, it was only a coincidence.

There was no intimation of that in the entire appellant's brief. That was because I was going to argue that the defendant's lawyer's lack of preparation produced this result, and I wanted the court to learn the details from the People's brief and not from me. But that just illustrates that there is no rule that hasn't got an exception.

So, that is my basic proposition as to the criminal appeal.

Let's turn to the civil. There, an appellant's problem is entirely different. The appellate courts have no great reluctance to taking responsibility in findings of fact. They do it all the time. In most civil disputes judges have no vested interest in protecting themselves from becoming involved in anything uncivilized. Indeed, I think most civil disputes are settled by arbitrators, mediators, and such without reference to any concept of due process of law. As a matter of fact, it is my belief that judges, although they think they are proud of the common-law heritage that distinguishes them from arbitrators and the like, are actually ashamed of the inordinate amount of time legal proceedings consume. Therefore, and again I am going to oversimplify, it is the appellant's job to make the court feel it is acting as an arbitrator who, in a Solomon-like fashion, clears up the errors below and sets the parties on some path more fruitful than continued litigation.

I had intended to illustrate this proposition with a discussion of several civil cases. Over the weekend, I decided to spare you all that. In the first place, I think the proposition is really self-evident. In the second place, civil cases are each so different in their special problems that it is difficult to generalize from them in a discussion of this kind, and discussion without generalization serves no purpose. So I shall, so to speak, submit that part of the argument on the brief.

Now that I have explained to you how you can't possibly lose either a civil or a criminal appeal, let us look briefly at two situations that don't seem to yield to the methods I have suggested. Suppose you have a civil case in which by no stretch of the imagination can you say justice, in any ultimate sense, is on your side and in which all you have is a technicality. For example, suppose that your opponent was three days late in serving his complaint, although your client knew all about the claim, and your only defense is the statute of limitations. Or, in a criminal case, suppose that the only substantial point that you can make is that the evidence does not justify the verdict. The only suggestion I have for such situations is that you should drain from your argument, both in brief and orally, every vestige of emotion and try to capture the court's interest in some intriguing intellectual proposition that you lay before it.

In saying this, I hasten to add that I have never been successful in that effort in a criminal case. I have had the problem only twice, *United States v Lawn* and *People v Corbo*, two of the cases listed in the pamphlet.

The defendant, Lawn, was a lawyer, and he had been a United States attorney in New Jersey. He got himself mixed up with some gangsters and, together with these gangsters, had been convicted of income tax conspiracy. I represented him on sentence. His trial attorney, Lloyd Paul Stryker, had died. In analyzing the cases for the sentence plea, I was convinced that the testimony of the government's principal witness, an accountant who had turned state's evidence and for whose veracity the government unhesitatingly vouched, actually exonerated my client; and that the so-called incriminating circumstances on which the government relied to tie him to the conspiracy could be conclusively refuted by the accountant's testimony.

I was also convinced that none of the procedural errors was of sufficient moment to get a reversal. I therefore concluded that the only possible approach to the appeal was to take the position which I have outlined and to urge that, as a matter of law, Lawn must be exonerated.

The threshold problem I met in succeeding with this approach was that when I explained it to my client, he got another lawyer. Perhaps he had heard this speech. The second half of my prophecy came true when the other lawyer, having analyzed the case differently, got all the way to the Supreme Court of the United States on a procedural point but there got only three judges to agree with him.

The other case, the *Corbo* case, represents perhaps the

worst fiasco in my professional life. Much of the wisdom, if you will indulge me by calling it that, that I have shared with you tonight comes from my ruminations about my fate in that case.

Mr. Corbo was a highly unsophisticated individual who had been convicted of murder. With his codefendant he had been hired by two thugs to collect a gambling debt from a certain butcher. The plan had been that the two defendants would jump into the butcher's car as he was leaving his place of business for the bank with the day's receipts, hold him up at the point of a gun, make him drive his car to a secluded place, and there relieve him of his money. The two gamblers who had hired the would-be robbers planned, of course, to follow them in their car so that the gamblers and not their hirelings would wind up with the $2,000 that the butcher was supposed to have.

Well, the butcher proved uncooperative. Instead of submitting and turning over his money, he grabbed the wheel, flung his hand on the horn, and put his foot on the accelerator; they were off. They went through the Bronx somewhat like a fire engine in a comedy.

Finally, the car ran into a wall, and the would-be robbers left their would-be victim and ran back to a car that was behind them, which they supposed to be their employers'. But, as you may have guessed, the gamblers, as soon as they saw that the plot wasn't going according to its script, had taken to the tall timbers. Their place in the line of march had been assumed by the ultimate deceased, an off-duty police officer who, going by in his own car, had seen the commotion and decided to follow and investigate.

Corbo, running back from the butcher's car, which he

had just abandoned, reached the policeman's car and started to get in. At that point the policeman grabbed Corbo's gun, which the latter still had in his hand. There was a tussle. The gun went off, and the policeman was killed.

There is no question in the world but that Corbo was guilty of manslaughter. The gun in his hand killed a policeman without justification. The question was: Was he guilty of murder in the first degree?

There was no evidence as to how the gun had gone off. All that was known was that there had been a tussle. The gun might have been made to fire by the policeman himself in his efforts to get it away from Corbo. There was no evidence whatever on the subject.

So the People came up with the theory of felony murder and accused Corbo of having entered the policeman's car with the intent to steal it. That theory was and is an absurdity. It should be obvious to anyone that Corbo had run back to that car expecting to find his employers, the gamblers who had hired him and were supposed to drive him and the loot away from the scene of the robbery, and that he had been the most surprised man in the world to find himself tussling with an off-duty policeman. But the judgment convicting him of murder in the first degree on the theory that he had tried to steal the policeman's car was unanimously affirmed by the Appellate Division and by the Court of Appeals.

What did I fail to do to make either court see the absurdity of the situation? The basic mistake, as I look back on it, was that I permitted myself to get emotional in the argument. I acted as though some basic injustice had been done to Corbo in convicting him of the higher degree of crime. As a matter of fact, there hadn't. It wasn't any credit to Corbo that he hadn't shot the butcher or somebody else in the course of the first robbery. So what had I to get excited about?

But I got excited. And in getting emotional, I marshaled against me all the instinctive advocacy that is in the breast of every judge, especially when you attack the essential procedures of which he is a part, as Harris Steinberg explained to you in a previous speech.

What I should have done was to drain my argument of all semblance of emotion and try to interest the court in a technical analysis of the evidence before it. Such an analysis would hopefully have demonstrated the absurdity of the result and deprived the People of their temporary success in sustaining their verdict.

Why do I say temporary? Well, there, alas, lies my personal fiasco. One of the arguments I deliberately did not raise was that certain alleged admissions by Corbo had been beaten out of him. The testimony concerning those admissions seemed to me patently fabricated, but I thought that the claim of police brutality was at best one for the jury and my experience with that kind of claim in the New York courts had been that it didn't predispose the court to listen to the rest of your argument.

So I eliminated that question. Well, other subsequently assigned counsel took a different view, and the United States Court of Appeals, in an opinion by Judge Lumbard, set aside the conviction on the ground of police brutality.

On that note of personal triumph, let's turn to the legislative appeal.

That is my personal designation for an appeal in which the particular interest of the client or party has relatively little or no importance in the outcome because the appellate court, moved by personal whim or overriding public necessity, wants to or must make new law.

In some cases of this type, there is nothing that a lawyer for either side can do to influence the outcome. Take, for example, the minimum wage cases, the first two listed in the pamphlet. In the first of these, the New York minimum wage law was declared invalid, 5 to 4. This was back in 1935.

In the second case, a year or so later, an identical Washington statute was held valid, again by 5 to 4. Mr. Justice Roberts had switched, the famous switch in time that saved nine. The switch was a matter of political necessity or conviction, and nothing any lawyer in either case had said or done could have had any effect on the outcome.

The same thing occurred with *Erie v Tompkins*, in which neither side made any contention that *Swift v Tyson* should be overruled, and also with *Mapp v Ohio*, in which, as Harris Steinberg told you, the appellant's lawyer didn't even mention *Wolf v Colorado*, the case he actually succeeded in having overruled.

But there are cases in this category in which counsel plays a definite role but not that of a conventional advocate. It is a role more akin to that of a legislative lobbyist. If you want inaction, if your client's interest lies in keeping the law as it is, don't worry the court about his particular problems but emphasize every consideration of a legislative character which will indicate that the time for change is not yet or that the instant case is not the appropriate field for change. If you want a change, if your client's interest is in new law, you must, of course, demonstrate why and how the change can be safely made.

I shall refer to only one of the cases I have listed in this category, *New York Times v Sullivan*. That's the case in which an Alabama public official got a verdict that, had it been upheld, would have precipitated suits against the *New York Times* totaling hundreds of millions of dollars. Now it didn't take an advocate to convince the Court that that case should be reversed. Anybody could see that a free press could not exist on a national basis if each of the fifty states could exercise effective censorship by imposition of its libel laws. The problem that confronted counsel for the *New York Times* was to contrive a theory of reversal, draft a statute, if you will, on which the majority of the justices would agree.

For example, because Mr. Justice Black wants altogether to abolish the action for libel and because a majority of his brethren not only know his views but violently dissent from them, any theory that would seem to head in that direction would run into extremely heavy sledding with at least seven of the justices. And similar difficulties could be conjured up with respect to almost any theory that could be suggested.

If you want a real intellectual treat, just block out for yourself all you know about the known objectives and preconceptions of the nine justices then sitting, and then study the opinion in the case against that background. You will get a real kick from the brilliant way counsel for the *Times* carried out their legislative assignment.

And that, Judge Breitel, is the end of my speech.

QUESTION PERIOD

QUESTION: Mr. Knapp, in a new development in criminal appeals, 813-c of the New York Code of Criminal Procedure permits us to appeal on the ground of violations of the Fourth or Fourteenth Amendment rights of the defendant after he has pleaded guilty. How can you persuade appellate judges that they should reverse a conviction because of these technical constitutional violations when there has been a confession of guilt in open court?

MR. KNAPP: Well, you have got to convince them that the violation of this process that the courts rely on to protect themselves from getting into the messy facts was so severe and so disruptive that the client had no choice but to plead guilty, that the plea of guilty was nothing but a formality of the trial. The violation was such that anything thereafter had to be a futility and therefore the court should now declare it so.

VOICE: May I make a suggestion to you, Mr. Knapp, on that point? Counsel who asked that question probably would experience no difficulty with a case under your theory in which he conceded the guilt of his client, whether the client had admitted guilt by a plea of guilty or by confession at the time of his arrest or whether he had been conclusively demonstrated to be guilty by the evidence introduced by the People. If your theory is correct, courts have no hesitation in overruling convictions, in fact, take some pleasure in overruling convictions, presumably just because of the strength of the evidence against them.

If I understood you correctly, you are not making any distinction between a strong and a weak case. The same considerations as to appellate tactics presumably would apply if the evidence was very strong against you that would apply if the evidence was intrinsically weak. Am I mistaken on that?

MR. KNAPP: You are correct on that, but you are not correct in the premise that you ascribe to me. I would never concede the guilt of the client. It's none of my business, and it's none of the court's business. It's between the client and God. This is a very serious distinction.

I do not propose to challenge the jury's right to find guilt on the basis of that evidence. I do propose to show that this particular jury never had a chance to decide that question according to the rules by which this particular judge and all his colleagues must live if they want to sleep at night.

JUDGE BREITEL: The question is interesting; without evaluating what the factual situations are that make an appellate court move in one direction or another, Mr. Knapp's analysis suggests that courts, with perhaps not as much courage as they should have or because of inhibitions imposed by the rules of their game, may find it necessary or expedient not to meet the question of doubt or accept it head on.

If you understand me and follow me, Mr. Knapp, what would you say to that?

MR. KNAPP: Well, my proposition is that the judges do not want to get themselves in the position of having to decide guilt or innocence.

Now I don't mean to suggest that any judge who consciously thinks that the defendant is innocent isn't going to find some way of declaring it, exactly as Frank Hogan would have raised a storm and dismissed the indictment if he had had any doubt that Dunn was guilty. But there is all the difference in the world between being personally convinced of an individual's guilt and being satisfied with a procedure that other people have followed.

The process by which we live, the judicial process, is geared so that each person takes his own responsibility. An appellate judge hasn't got time to go into all the records that come before him and take the responsibility for deciding the guilt or innocence of each defendant. If he tried to do that, his civil work would end and so would he. All he can do is look at the record and see whether the people who decided that question or the people who participated in the decision acted according to the rules.

Now, of course, there will be some cases that will be so clear that they will supervene this rule on either side. In some cases, the evidence is so clear that you can't conceive that the particular error which you are complaining of could have affected the result. In such a case, the appellant can be as ingenious as he wants but he won't get anywhere.

I mentioned the fact that I was in court the other day and heard the argument I have discussed. Well, the case I was in court to argue is now on its way to the Court of Appeals, and there were no dissents. So there are some cases in which guilt is so clear that the court won't do anything about it, no matter whether you can come up with error or not.

There are some cases in which innocence is equally clear, but very few of them. The police, as a matter of fact, don't usually get the wrong man, and if they do, the district attorney usually finds out before the case comes to trial, and if he doesn't find out before it comes to trial, he usually finds out before it goes to appeal.

But to give you an illustration of an apparent exception to the rule, take *People v Caruso*, the first case mentioned in the pamphlet. Now that case would seem to contradict everything I have told you, because the appellant argued nothing substantial except the defendant's innocence.

The defendant was an illiterate Italian. His baby got diphtheria and died. The doctor who had been treating the baby was two hours late. The doctor was two hours late after an emergency call and came an hour or so after the baby had died. The father was crying and singing to the dead baby in his arms when the doctor came in. The doctor, learning that the baby had died, made some facial grimace which the defendant mistook for laughter. The defendant thereupon dropped the baby and choked the doctor, dragged him into the kitchen, got out a carving knife, and slit his throat; and that was the end of the doctor.

Now that case was briefed, among others, by Howard Spellman, and even in those days he was interested in divorce and divorced his client from the electric chair. But the brief said nothing about anything, except that on this evidence you could not say that Caruso had intended to kill.

Although that is an apparent exception to my rule, like a good many exceptions it actually proves the rule, because the defendant did not challenge anything that the People had proved. As a matter of fact, whoever represented the defendant at trial must have been a genius because he did not plead insanity, which would be the natural thing to do. He put in no defense at all. All he did was to put the client on the stand and let the client tell in substance the same story that he had told to the district attorney.

Well, the jury convicted him, but you can see that this case could be put before the court with no controversy, and that's what I am getting at. If you put the case before the court with controversy, you build up the advocate who's in the court, and as Harris Steinberg explained to you (and this applies to civil cases to some extent), the court is part of the establishment and instinctively defends the establishment. That's just a fact of life.

This case was put before the court with no advocacy, just a statement of the dramatic fact, and the court couldn't bring itself to affirm the judgment of conviction.

If you want to read a beautiful opinion, read this one by Judge Andrews. It just seethes with the pathos that caused the court to reverse the conviction.

So this on its surface would be contrary to what I just said, but in actuality it proves my point through an exception.

QUESTION: If as a point of advocacy you do not want to appeal to any question of justice in a criminal appeal, are there considerations of justice in ordinary nonlegislative civil appeals that you can use effectively as an advocate on appeal, depending on whether you want to persuade the court that justice was done or that it was not done?

MR. KNAPP: I dislike the use of the word "justice" because in this context it is highly inexact. I certainly don't want to leave the impression that you are not supposed to appeal to justice in a criminal appeal, but the justice that you appeal to is the right of a man to be tried according to the rules, because if he is not tried according to the rules, the judge can't sleep at night. The judge has got to reverse. He can't take the responsibility for affirming in a case in which a man was not tried according to the rules. How can he say that if the rules had been followed, the result would have been the same?

Now it's immaterial whether the man was innocent or guilty, because the judge hasn't got the time or the energy to get himself involved in that question. So in a criminal appeal, the injustice you cry about is that the rules were violated in such a way that the judges cannot go home and sleep if they affirm, because of the fear that a proper application of the rules might have brought about a different result.

In the case I mentioned concerning too many lawyers (I read you an excerpt from my brief), the prevailing opinion by Judge Bastow makes it quite clear that he had no personal belief that the man was innocent. But Judge Bastow said (he didn't use these words), "I can't tell what the jury would have done if the man had had his rights; so I am not going to let the verdict stand."

In a civil case your appeal should be to justice as the term is more generally used. A result in this case is not what the testator expected, if it's a will case. It's not what the parties expected, if it's a contract case. It's not what the Legislature expected, if it's a statutory-interpretation case.

But by and large in civil cases the appellate court doesn't really care, unless a really outrageous thing has been done, how the result was achieved if the net result is what the parties were entitled to expect. Even then it doesn't do the appellant any good just to show that the result is not quite right, because the courts have a very sound feeling that it's much better for the people to get their disputes done with and go on to work and earn a living in some other way.

So, in a civil case, if you don't show that the result was really wrong, it is going to be affirmed. That's what I mean by the difference. In each case you ask for justice, but you ask for it in a different way.

JUDGE BREITEL: One thing is obvious: advocacy is changing. In the old days they taught you how to keep the judges awake on the bench. Now the rule is how to put them to sleep at night!

QUESTION: Mr. Knapp, haven't you really loaded paradox on paradox when you suggest that because of the court's identification with the establishment, because of its commitment to the system, it has venerated obedience to the rules and procedures of a criminal case above the result? Aren't you saying, in effect, that the distrust that the appellate court has shown for the manner in which the trial court, the jury, and the prosecutor have performed their functions, as evidenced by the multiplication of posttrial remedies, all of which look behind the court's integrity, all of which look to the manner in which the police officer has conducted his investigation and, in effect, challenge the process, illustrates a suspicion rather than a veneration for the establishment of which the appellate court is a part?

MR. KNAPP: Your question is clear, but it gets two things confused. The proliferation of post-conviction procedures is not the product of the state appellate courts but of the Supreme Court in Washington, and that is a subject of legislative appeals. It has nothing to do with criminal appeals.

Coram nobis came about because (a) a certain person had to be got out of jail and (b) the Court of Appeals had some feeling of the requirements of constitutional change that were on the horizon. But this proliferation of post-conviction procedures is entirely in response to what I call legislative decisions—and I am not being critical of action in Washington—and not, to my knowledge, in response to any feeling of distrust that our courts feel about our procedures.

I do not wish to give the impression that any judge, consciously or unconsciously, is uninterested in the result. But the rules of life as well as of law being what they are, he cannot undertake to make a personal appraisal of the result in every criminal case that comes before him. If he did undertake to do so, he would soon do nothing else but consider criminal appeals and the civil calendar would get even more clogged than it is now. Furthermore, he would have a nervous breakdown.

What he can do is see to it that the rules are followed and that the jury has had an opportunity to make an unprejudiced appraisal of the facts. Then if the situation does not seem absurd, he will feel confident in letting it stand.

JUDGE BREITEL: I am finally teased into making some comment on my own behalf. I warned Mr. Knapp in advance, not really intending to fulfill the warning, that I would rebut him on anything that he said during the evening.

I don't agree with Mr. Knapp that judges do not try to test the fact of innocence or guilt in a criminal case or, in a civil case, do not test the fact that the judgment rendered is right or wrong, despite the risk of sleeplessness and the risk of enhancing the burdens that they have. As a matter of fact, if anything there is a greater danger that judges, in their anxiety, will depart from the rules of the game, from what has been provided for them by the advocates, and decide, on some basis not supportable by the record or the law or even by reason, that a person is innocent or guilty or that a civil case is right or wrong as it has been decided. As I say that, I recognize that judges may vary, although my experience is that this practice is fairly common among them.

For example, Judge Botein has often been quoted as saying that judges need time to brood. I suggest that that is not universally true. Some need time to brood, and some don't. So some may be searching for the essential justice or rightness of a result in a case, and others may not.

There is a very important truth, however, in what Mr. Knapp has said tonight, and that truth is the one that he has irritated me with over the years. It is that there is a difference, contrary to what we expect, in the approach to the criminal case as compared with the approach to the civil and, too, that there is a special problem of why a court chooses one method rather than another for the purpose of upsetting or affirming the results, civil or criminal.

So it disturbs me no end that the vast bulk of criminal cases which are reversed are reversed precisely on the ground that Mr. Knapp has set forth. The result usually does turn on rules of procedure.

This is not inconsistent with what I said. I still think that most judges will look to the essential rightness, the innocence or guilt, in a criminal case. And yet when they come to rationalize, to explain their decision, they will do what Mr. Knapp says they do.

Now, this suggests some very, very fundamental problems in the whole judicial process. The answers are not found so simply in the writings of the past, and I doubt if they are found simply in the comments tonight. I am sure Mr. Knapp will agree with that.

I didn't mean to deliver the peroration here. That's not my purpose or my function, but he did irritate me enough, which is what he always does. By the way, that's how he got that extra vote in the closely divided *Douglas* case, because when he went into court that day, the best he had was two votes. In fact, I am not sure he had that many. But he was irritating enough with these devious, indirect methods of his and his refusal to discuss the innocence or guilt of the defendant (and here I prove his case for him) that he got my vote.

QUESTION: I was thinking that perhaps there isn't as much difference between the criminal and the civil appeals as appears superficially. "Rules of procedure" means something different in a criminal case from what it means in a civil case—so many days to serve a summons, and so forth. The so-called rules of procedure in a criminal case are sometimes more fundamental than the substantive rules in civil trials, and that's the reason why the courts more frequently reverse on rules of procedure in criminal cases.

MR. KNAPP: That's really another way, perhaps a more orthodox way, of saying what I have been saying this evening. Just by way of comment, I assume that this audience is sophisticated enough not to think that I have tried to give them the whole truth in an hour or that I have indicated how every appeal should be argued.

With respect to the chairman's comments, he of course feels that I have overstated the case, which, indeed, I have. But I just leave you with this overall observation, which I deeply feel to be valid. In criminal cases, appellate judges have an underlying—unconscious, if you will—reluctance to involve themselves in responsibility for ultimate decision and a corresponding desire to be assured that, because all proprieties were observed in the decision-making process, they are entitled to rely on decisions made by others. In civil cases, on the other hand, appellate judges have a quite conscious desire to get to the root of the matter before them and bring controversy to an end and no reluctance whatever to involve themselves in ultimate decision. It is the advocate's function to be aware of these tendencies and to exploit them to his client's advantage.

References Made by Mr. Knapp to Pamphlet Distributed

CRIMINAL APPEALS

People v Caruso (1927) 246 NY 437, 150 NE 390

People v Ludkowitz (1935) 266 NY 233, 194 NE 688

People v Bartelini (1941) 285 NY 433, 35 NE2d 29

People v Dunn (1948) 298 NY 564, 84 NE2d 635, *cert den*, 336 US 946

People v Kelly (1951) 302 NY 512, 99 NE2d 552

People v Corbo (1st Dept 1954) 284 App Div 273, 131 NYS2d 540, *aff'd* 307 NY 928, 123 NE2d 574 *cert den*, 348 US 977

People v Corbo (1st Dept 1962) 17 App Div 2d 351, 234 NYS2d 662

Lawn v United States (1958) 355 US 339

United States *ex rel* Corbo v LaVallee (2d Cir 1959) 270 F2d 513

People v Douglas (1st Dept 1963) 19 App Div 2d 455, 244 NYS2d 55

People v Ramirez (1st Dept 1960) 12 App Div 2d 607, 217 NYS2d 501, *aff'd*, 10 NY2d 774, 177 NE2d 56

People v Richardson (1st Dept 1966) 25 App Div 2d 221, 268 NYS2d 419

CIVIL APPEALS

In re United Cigar Stores Co. of America (2d Cir 1937) 89 F2d 3

Colodney *v* New York Coffee & Sugar Exchange (Spec Term, NY Co 1956) 1 Misc 2d 643, *rev'd*, 1 App Div 2d 999, 151 NYS2d 705, *aff'd*, 2 NY2d 149, 138 NE2d 810

Colodney *v* New York Coffee & Sugar Exchange (1st Dept 1957) 4 App Div 2d 137, 163 NYS2d 283, *aff'd*, 4 NY2d 698, 138 NE2d 810

Jackson *v* Hunt, Hill & Betts (1959) 7 NY2d 180, 196 NYS2d

Matter of Wise (Surr NY Co 1962) 37 Misc 2d 403, *mod*, 20 App Div 2d 55, 244 NYS2d 960, *aff'd*, 15 NY2d 591, 202 NE2d 563

Matter of McDonnell (1st Dept 1965) 23 App Div 2d 729, 257 NYS2d 689

LEGISLATIVE APPEALS

West Coast Hotel Co. *v* Parrish (1937) 300 US 379, *overruling* Morehead *v* New York (1935) 298 US 587

Erie *v* Tompkins (1938) 304 US 64, *overruling* Swift *v* Tyson (1842) 41 US (16 Pet) 1

Fay *v* New York (1947) 332 US 261

Doubleday & Co. *v* New York (1948) 335 US 848

Stemmer *v* New York (1949) 336 US 963

Mapp *v* Ohio (1961) 367 US 643, *overruling* Wolf *v* Colorado (1949) 338 US 25

Merritt-Chapman & Scott Corp. *v* Public Utility District (SDNY 1962) 207 F Supp 443, *rev'd*, (2d Cir 1963) 319 F2d 94, *on remand*, (SDNY 1965) 237 F Supp 985

New York Times *v* Sullivan (1964) 376 US 254

Mr. Knapp refers to *People v Richardson*, p. 79

SUPREME COURT

APPELLATE DIVISION—FIRST DEPARTMENT

February 1966

Bernard Botein, P. J.,
Charles D. Breitel,
Benjamin J. Rabin,
Samuel W. Eager,
Earle C. Bastow, JJ.

The People of the State of New York,
Respondent,

vs.

Willie Richardson and Charles Wade,
Defendants-Appellants.

Appeal from judgments of the Supreme Court of the State of New York, County of New York (Sarafite, J.) rendered March 31, 1964, upon a verdict convicting defendants of Robbery in the First Degree.

George B. Adams, Jr. of counsel (Anthony F. Marra, attorney) for appellants.

Alan F. Leibowitz of counsel (Michael Juviler with him on the brief; Frank S. Hogan, District Attorney) for respondent.

RABIN, J.:

Defendants, Willie Richardson and Charles Wade, were convicted of Robbery in the First Degree. At the trial, the People relied primarily on the testimony of the victim, one Chong, a Chinese waiter, who testified as follows: On July 16, 1963, at around 1:30 A.M. he returned from his job to his home in the Alfred E. Smith project, and was followed into the elevator of the building in which he resides by three young men. When the elevator reached the eighth floor, two of the men left. The third man continued to the tenth floor where Chong lives and, as Chong stepped out of the elevator, he was attacked by the third man. The other two men then rejoined the third and participated in the attack. Chong's jacket was pulled over his head and he was struck with a hard object. Twenty dollars was removed from his wallet. The attackers then fled.

At the trial, Chong identified the appealing defendants, Richardson and Wade, and the defendant Bowie as his attackers.

On the same day of the attack, Chong was taken to the Housing Authority's police office, and he there identified, first Wade and Bowie, and later on, Richardson. At the trial, it was brought out that at the hearing in Criminal Court, Chong testified that the police officer pointed to Richardson when he asked Chong whether Richardson was one of those involved in the robbery. However, Chong denied that this had been done. The People rested its case solely on the testimony of Chong. The defense, through the testimony of Detective Stern, cast some doubt on the identification of the defendants by Chong, in that soon after the robbery occurred, Chong, upon being questioned could give only a vague description of his assailants, indicating only their approximate height and race, and also indicating that he would not be able to recognize his assailants if he saw them again.

After the defense called defendant Wade's mother, and a character witness for defendant Bowie, the defense rested. The People, thereupon, moved to reopen its case, which motion was granted. The People called Grantley Crichlow, a guard for the New York City Housing Authority. Crichlow testified that on July 11, 1963, at about 11:30 P.M., he saw three young men sitting on a bench near the project. The men were identified by the witness as the three defendants. Crichlow stated that he saw the three men again around 1:00 A.M. on July 16, and indicated that a fourth was present. Crichlow also stated that he saw the three enter the premises occupied by Chong, at around 1:20 A.M., but did not recall seeing Chong enter the premises. It was brought out, however, that Crichlow, after hearing of the commission of the crime during the same tour of duty, did nothing until the evening of July 16, when he returned to duty and then spoke to Patrolman Phipps of the Housing Authority police.

Patrolman Phipps was called by the People and testified that he observed four youths acting in a disorderly manner, and ordered them to disperse. About one hour later, at 12:30–1:00 A.M., on July 16, 1963, the four returned to the area of the premises involved. Phipps also testified to a conversation he had with the defendants, after he had placed them under arrest, and after Chong had identified the defendants. Phipps testified that as he brought the defendants to the Criminal Court, and as he was placing them in the cell, immediately prior to their arraignment, he asked the defendants if they could tell him "who was the fourth party who walked away with the suitcase just before the robbery was committed." The defendants Richardson, and Wade, replied that they would "think about it, we'll let you know * * *".

It is our opinion that the admission into evidence of such inculpatory statements, made at a time when arraignment was about to take place, was improper, and in the circumstances of the case, constitutes reversible error. There is no doubt that the statements were inculpatory. The defendants' contention at the trial was that at the time the crime was committed, they were not in the area. The statements attributed to the defendants by patrolman Phipps could have indicated quite to the contrary, that the defendants were in the area.

The recent decisions in the area compel a finding that the statements were not admissible. In *People* v. *Meyer*, 11 NY 2d 162, where the defendant had been informed, upon arraignment, of his right to counsel, and requested none, the Court held:

> "An arraignment after an arrest must be deemed the first stage of a criminal proceeding. * * * In reason and logic the admissibility into evidence of a post-arraignment statement should not be treated any differently than a post-indictment statement. A statement so taken necessarily impinges on the fundamentals of protection against testimonial compulsion, since the jury might well accord it weight beyond its worth to reach a verdict of guilty. * * * We thus conclude that any statement made by an accused after arraignment not in the presence of counsel as in *Spano*, *DiBiasi*, and *Waterman* (*supra*) is inadmissible." (p. 164–5)

The *Meyer* rule was followed in *People* v. *Rodriguez*, 11 NY 2d 279, where there was a sworn information charging the defendant with first degree murder. The defendant was brought before a Justice of the Peace where the charge was read to him. However, the arraignment proceedings were adjourned. Some hours before the postponed arraignment was held, the defendant was questioned by the police and he confessed. The Court held such confession inadmissible, stating that "[i]t is the interrogation, in the absence of counsel, after the criminal proceeding has been commenced, whether by grand jury indictment or by a charge placed before a magistrate following an arrest, which is forbidden." (p. 284)

We cannot see any reason or logic which would compel a distinction between this case and People v. Rodriguez, supra. While the statements were made prior to arraignment, they were made in the courthouse with the arraignment imminent —the defendants being held in the cell in the courthouse, waiting for their case to be called. The judicial process therefore, had in effect, begun. We are of the belief that at the time the statements were made, the defendants were entitled to counsel.

We note that the Meyer principle has been applied to pre-arraignment statements. In People v. Fleischmann, 43 Misc. 2d 200 (cited with approval in People v. Bodie, 16 NY 2d 275), the complainant swore to a complaint charging the defendant with the theft of an automobile, and thereafter a warrant of arrest was issued. The defendant, upon being questioned ten (10) days after the issuance of the warrant, confessed to the crime. The Court held the evidence inadmissible since the judicial process had been invoked. It was, as is here, the People's contention that since the statements were not post-arraignment statements, the defendant's constitutional rights were not violated.

We agree with the analysis in People v. Fleischmann. The rationale of the Meyer and Rodriguez decisions is "that a confession or admission made after the *commencement of a judicial proceeding* on a charge relating to the confession or admission is not admissible in evidence if such confession or admission was made in the absence of counsel. * * * [O]nce the judicial process has been invoked* * * judicial concern for the defendant's rights makes his interrogation in the absence of counsel 'an impermissible step in the progress of the criminal cause'." (*People* v. *Fleischmann*, at p. 201. See also *People* v. *Santmyer*, 20 App Div 2d, 960).

As noted, we feel the rule enunciated in *Meyer, supra,* is applicable here. The situation is not unlike that in *Rodriguez*, where the arraignment had begun but was postponed and continued at a later date. To distinguish this case, where the defendants were awaiting arraignment, would be to put form over substance. Defendants were at a point far past the investigatory, or accusatory stage—in fact, they were then defendants in the courthouse awaiting trial, and therefore their constitutional right to counsel should be deemed to have attached. Thus, the inculpatory statements were inadmissible.

We note, too, that the inculpatory statements were not merely cumulative in their evidentiary effect. The accuracy of the identification by the witness, Chong, was cast in doubt. The testimony of the other identifying witnesses merely placed the defendants in the area, and indeed contained certain discrepancies. Each of the defendants claimed alibis, and hence the inculpatory statements could have shifted the weight of the evidence in the minds of the jurors.

In passing, we also find it necessary to comment on the conduct of the District Attorney in the presentation of his case, resulting in the reopening of the People's, as well as the defendants' case. On this appeal, the District Attorney stated that defendant Bowie's opening statement indicated that Bowie, and an alibi witness, would be called to the stand. However, neither Bowie nor his proposed witness took the stand by the time the defense rested. It is argued that the prosecution had been saving the two Housing Authority officers to rebut the expected alibi testimony. While we do not hold that the Court, in furtherance of justice, should not have allowed the reopening of the People's case, we feel constrained to note that the prosecution's attempt at gaining a tactical advantage was not justified. The testimony of the officers who saw the defendants in the area at the time of the crime, should have been presented on the People's direct case and not held for rebuttal. It is the duty of the People to present the full case on which it relies to the jury. Moreover, the tactics used could be deemed to have prejudiced the defendants considerably, for the alibis offered by the defense—when it reopened its case—appeared to be an afterthought. The Prosecutor should not be allowed to so subvert the presentation of the evidence as was here done.

Accordingly, the judgment is reversed on the law and the facts and a new trial ordered.

All concur.

NOTE

In discussing the "legislative appeal," I referred to *Morehead v New York* and *West Coast Hotel Co. v Parrish*, the cases in which Mr. Justice Roberts switched sides, as illustrating my point that in some situations counsel can do nothing to affect the results.

After the speech, I discovered in *Roosevelt and Frankfurter*, Little, Brown and Company, Boston, 1967, pp. 393–395, a memorandum by Mr. Justice Roberts, in which he asserts that precisely the opposite was the case. He states, in substance, that he voted with the majority in *Morehead* solely because counsel for New York had not asked for a reconsideration of *Adkins v Children's Hospital*, but had sought, unsuccessfully, in Justice Roberts' opinion, to distinguish it; and that he had voted with the majority in *West Coast Hotel Co.* because counsel for the state of Washington had asked for reconsideration of *Adkins* and had convinced him it should be overruled.

In commenting upon the memorandum, Mr. Justice Frankfurter observed that it was regrettable that Mr. Justice Roberts had not made his position clear in the published reports of the two cases. *Whitman Knapp*

Hot Bench or Cold Bench

When the Court Has or Has Not Read
the Brief before Oral Argument

SAMUEL E. GATES

Samuel E. Gates, a partner in the firm of Debevoise, Plimpton, Lyons and Gates of New York City, is a fellow of the American College of Trial Lawyers. Educated at the University of Southern California (A.B., M.A., LL.B.), he is a graduate also of the Institut des Hautes Etudes Internationales, University of Paris. He has been active in international aviation affairs and appellate litigation. A member of The Association of the Bar of the City of New York, he belongs also to the American Bar Association, the American Law Institute, and the American Society of International Law.

When I was first assigned the topic "Hot Bench or Cold Bench," I hoped it might have a little sex appeal. As I got further into the matter, I concluded that that emotional appeal was lacking. I felt a little like Ulysses sailing between Scylla and Charybdis. I soon came to realize that however I might treat the subject tonight, I would be in hot water with some of you and probably be greeted with icy reserve by the rest. I will add that I did have confidence that I would not, on this occasion, be speaking to a tepid, or lukewarm, bench, and that sometimes does happen. Perhaps I shall say a little about what I call a "tepid" court later in this discussion. I should say at the outset that because there is such a wide and often strong divergence of views on the subject, when I make allusions to particular examples, any similarity between those examples and any of the appellate tribunals before which I appear is entirely coincidental.

In this series of discussions you have heard talks on the criminal appeal, the civil appeal, and a comparison between them. I think these topics call for a more philosophical approach than does my subject, and for that reason I intend to deal with my subject somewhat more pragmatically.

I approach this subject with some reticence, first, because many experienced appellate advocates are present, and second, because of the elusiveness of the subject matter itself. The structure and presentation of an oral argument, particularly on appeal, are one of the most difficult tasks facing a lawyer. The average lawyer has relatively little experience before an appellate tribunal; many never argue an appeal throughout their entire professional careers. Chief Judge Lumbard of the Second Circuit, in a recent speech before the New York State Bar, deplored the decline in the performance of the appellate bar, saying that in his experience not more than one out of ten cases is well argued. I suppose this is not surprising when we examine another figure which he used: of 758 arguments of counsel in a single term, 625 were made by lawyers who appeared only once that year.

The argument of an appeal is peculiarly an individual matter: what works for one lawyer will not work for another, and what proves successful before one appellate court falls like a lead balloon before another. As John Dewey puts it, "You learn by doing." To attempt to tell another how best to prepare and to argue an appeal, before a bench of whatever temperature, is like trying to tell someone how to ride a bicycle—it just can't be done. You've got to get out and do it, even if you get banged up a little in the process. There are, of course, some general rules that all of us should follow. Every lawyer who argues an appeal should first read some of the literature in this area: to mention just a few, the speeches by Prof. Karl Llewellyn and Mr. Justice Jackson, Whitman Knapp's fine piece in the *Record*, and Colonel Wiener's comprehensive book *Briefing and Arguing Federal Appeals*.

A brief reference to some of the ground rules with respect to preparing and arguing an appeal is essential as background for our topic tonight, and no better compendium of these rules—they might almost be called the ten commandments of appellate argument—can be found than that classic speech given before this same forum twenty-six years ago by John W. Davis. I commend it to you. It is printed in Volume 26 of the *ABA Journal*. It would ill become me to attempt to improve upon such an illustrious appellate advocate as Mr. Davis. I can perhaps best illustrate my feelings about doing such a thing by telling you a story attributed to Chief Justice Traynor of the California Supreme Court. A young lawyer was arguing a question of California state law which had not been decided in that state. The leading decision against him had been written by Mr. Justice Holmes while he was on the Supreme Judicial Court of Massachusetts. At the moment when the young lawyer was reaching the zenith of his criticism of Justice Holmes's reasoning, there came one of those earth tremors—as an ex-Californian I must say that the word "earthquake" has been banned from my vocabulary—for which the state is famous, whereupon one of the judges leaned across the bench and said, "That's Justice Holmes stirring in protest."

I will mention at the outset only a few of those cardinal rules which to me are the *sine qua non* of the art of appellate persuasion, whether before a hot bench or a cold bench.

First, never miss an opportunity to present oral argument by following the easy course of saying "Submitted." An apt simile has often been used: it's a lot more difficult to persuade a pretty young thing to say "Yes" by letter than by the spoken word; in the latter case you can see the glint of approbation or the frown of a prospective negative and, if necessary, change your tactic in order to get that "Yes."

Second, learn all you can about the members of the panel before whom you are to appear. Appellate advocacy is the art of persuasion, and it is your job to persuade every member of that panel—three, five, seven, or even nine men—of the justice of your client's cause. The more you know about them and their backgrounds, the more likely it is that you can touch a responsive chord. Believe it or not, appellate judges are human beings. They suffer the infirmities and enjoy the strengths of other people; some are quick, others slow. All have been influenced by their environment and their experiences; they have their predilections and emotions, even as you and I. For example, suppose a young man's father has lost everything in an involuntary bankruptcy that they both feel was unjustified. As a result, the young man was forced to skimp and scrape to get an education. In later years, as a judge, this same young man is not likely to be sympathetic to appeals predicated on the sufferings of a bankrupt's creditors.

You have heard references in past lectures to Mr. Davis's comparing the judges to fish for whom you are angling. I am not sure I ought to carry the analogy any further, but I am sure that you don't generally catch a fast-moving trout with a chunk of soggy bread, and I'm equally sure you don't get a sucker with a dry fly. I know too that if all the panel were former prosecuting attorneys, you would probably get a reaction different in almost every case from what it would be if their earlier training had been in Legal Aid or in representing large corporations.

It may surprise you, but many firms keep "book" on all

the judges before whom they appear. This book includes much more than a biographical sketch which you might find in *Who's Who:* Does the judge listen with patience, or does he seem absorbed in other matters or half asleep? Does he treat the government as just another litigant, or does the government have a preferred or, sometimes, a prejudiced position? Does he seem impressed by the reputation or prestige of the lawyer making the argument? These and many other impressions are recorded for future reference.

Third, know your record from cover to cover. If it's a lengthy record that you can't remember, have it indexed and key portions of the transcript and exhibits tabbed or marked so you can quickly find what you want. I know of nothing better calculated to lose the attention of the court and break the pace of your argument than to have a lengthy pause, the silence broken only by the shuffling of a stack of papers, while you try to locate a pertinent part of the record or a misplaced exhibit.

Fourth, be flexible. Too often an appellate lawyer comes into court with his argument carved in granite, and no matter what happens during the argument, he tries to follow it to the bitter end. Mr. Davis said, "Rejoice when the court asks questions. And again I say unto you, rejoice!" Questions at least assure you that the inquiring judge is not asleep. But more important, a question gives you some idea of how the court is thinking and an opportunity to dispel any uncertainties about your position. Answer the question then and there. Never say, "I'll come to that matter later in my argument." That isn't when the judge wants the answer; he may forget the context of his question or, worse, make up his mind before you get to that point, or your time may run out without the answer's having been given. It may be that the answer deserves much more attention than you feel can be given at the time of the question, but at least give a summary answer before saying, "I shall treat that matter at greater length later in my argument." Ideally, you should be so thoroughly prepared that mentally you can rearrange your entire argument and treat the question in the depth it deserves. That question, notwithstanding all your careful planning, may be the "jugular vein" of the case.

Fifth, never read your argument. And it goes without saying that your argument should not be just a rehash or a summarization of your brief. Perhaps you will lose some of the mellifluous phraseology of the written text, and your sentence structure may leave something to be desired, but your argument will be infinitely more effective. You cannot keep your nose buried in the manuscript of an argument and at the same time watch for that flicker of interest in the judges' eyes which may be of telltale importance. That's not possible even with bifocals. In this connection I probably should add that Rule 44 of the United States Supreme Court Rules says: "The court looks with disfavor on any oral argument that is read from a prepared text."

This leads naturally to an observation. I'm afraid that much too frequently lawyers are retained to argue appeals solely because of their prestige and reputation. Often it is difficult for a lawyer who has not been intimately involved in the preparation and trial of a case, in the time available, to get a complete grasp of all its ramifications. At one time I taught public speaking. I quickly learned that the man who talked on a subject he knew—it might be about his leading a boy scout troop or building a brick wall—usually made a far better and more interesting speech than the one who chose some impressive or erudite subject about which he had only a smattering of information. The same thing is true in an appellate argument. A young man making his first argument who has an intimate knowledge of the facts and applicable law will probably make a more effective argument than the "name" advocate hired to impress the bench.

So much for what I consider fundamentals. I suppose I also should say at this point that I have no intention of announcing now or at the end of this discussion that I think the hot bench is better or worse than the cold bench. Only a braver and more persuasive man than I would be so venturesome. But there is a difference between the two benches, and I should like to explore with you the consequences for the advocate that flow from these differences and perhaps suggest some ways of coping with those consequences.

Before doing so, I think we should define what we mean by "hot" and "cold" benches. Let's take the cold bench first, for that's somewhat easier. The judges have read neither the briefs nor the record; they know nothing of the case, unless it is one of the few highly publicized cases that reach the newspapers—a *Dr. Sheppard* or a *Texas Gulf Sulphur* case—and represent less than 1 percent of all appellate cases. The judges have no preconceived notions as to how your case should be decided. They listen to your argument with an open mind.

By contrast, a hot bench, in the narrow sense, is one

on which all the judges have read the briefs and the salient parts of the record. The court, therefore, is generally familiar with the facts and the legal issues and has devoted some time to thinking about the case, perhaps even to the point of jotting down questions. There is, of course, the in-between practice followed by a few courts of assigning a single judge the task of reading the briefs and record before argument and giving him primary responsibility for the questioning. With respect to this arrangement, I have no reluctance in expressing an opinion: I don't like it. I don't like it because too often the argument becomes a discussion between counsel and this one judge while his colleagues sit back as interested onlookers, deriving little or no benefit from the interchange.

But the definition of a hot bench that I have just given is probably too narrow. Obviously, if the appellate tribunal reviewed your case at some prior stage in the proceedings, it must be considered hot. Likewise, if the court has had a good deal of experience in the area of law in which your case falls, I am inclined to classify that bench also as hot. Judge Learned Hand, for example, was famous for the saltiness of his admiralty opinions. And the Court of Appeals for the District of Columbia is certainly hot in cases concerning administrative law.

The best example of the cold bench made hot by experience concerns a law professor who had been employed by a state administrative agency to argue its appeals. In two cases raising precisely the same issue of law, the regulatory agency had come to opposite conclusions. In spite of every effort to get the cases set at different times or before different judges, the lawyer found himself scheduled to argue the two cases back to back before the same court. So, mindful of his duty as an advocate, he rose to his feet at the appointed time and argued the first case on behalf of the appellant. Then, at the conclusion of the opening argument in the second case, he began to argue the other side of the same issue on behalf of the appellee. After a few minutes of the second argument he was interrupted by one of the judges, who said, "Pardon me, counsel, perhaps I haven't understood you correctly; is there any way that you can win both of these cases?" "No, your Honor," came the answer, "but I don't see how I can lose both of them either." Thereupon the judge replied, "Well, counsel, I suppose that's better than your usual average."

In another situation, if the bench is not hot, it is very warm: when, even if the court has not reviewed the precise legal issue in the past, it has decided cases that contained closely related issues. Legal principles have a tendency to fall into large categories, and the issues in those categories have much in common. For example, the law with respect to the fiduciary obligations owed by corporate directors has been evolving with a quickened pace these last few years. If you are preparing to argue a case that goes somewhat further than any decided case, you should be intimately familiar with the way in which the members of your court have treated other fiduciary relationships in similar contexts and so be able to ascertain the direction in which the panel is moving. In oral argument you have an opportunity to carry the members of the panel over that last hurdle or to raise the hurdle to new heights, as the case may be, that is not available in the written brief. It is important to know whether your judges are sensitive to fiduciary duties in a commercial setting or are more impressed with the "business" aspects of such dealings.

Over the years every judge develops more or less settled attitudes toward fundamental issues of this character, attitudes that he has come to through long experience and thought. I should go further: not only judges but entire courts develop more or less settled attitudes, and these attitudes change from time to time as the makeup of the courts change. For example, it is my observation that the New York Court of Appeals is what I might term "law-oriented" (apt to follow traditional lines) while the First Department seems to be much more "trial-court oriented." It is important that you focus on these attitudes, for in analyzing them you will be assisted in casting your arguments in the most effective way.

Why is the hotness or the coldness of the bench important? It is perfectly obvious that if the court has read the record and briefs, both the amount and the precision of the questioning from the bench will be increased and the advocate must be all the more flexible in the presentation of his case. But what is too little appreciated, I think, is that if the court has thoroughly familiarized itself with the factual and legal issues, the whole function of the appellate argument changes, and this fact has very important consequences for the appellate lawyer.

With a cold bench, you are writing on a clean slate, at least insofar as the facts are concerned. The initiative lies almost wholly with counsel. The lawyer is given the opportunity of drawing the facts and applicable law in a way most favorable to his client; and if he does his job properly, this first impression will not be forgotten. When the judges subsequently read the briefs, which usually occurs at any time up to three weeks after the argument, the reading will take place in light of the impressions formed at oral argument, and those impressions should include an answer for the major contentions raised in your opponent's brief.

Even in an argument before a cold bench, the advocate probably will be subject to questions, and as I have said, you should welcome them. You then and there have the opportunity to persuade or dissuade. But by and large the questions raised will be only those precipitated by your oral presentation. Without an opportunity to reflect on both sides of the case, the court will find it difficult to go much beyond the facts and issues that you present in your argument. And the relatively short period of time most courts allow for argument means that if you are the appellant, you will have completed your argument before the court comes to grips with the central issues.

If you are the respondent-appellee, you are likely to be subject to more questioning, but even then the issues will tend to be those raised by the argument itself, and again your time is likely to be used before the court has had much of an opportunity to think about the basic points at issue.

I suggest to you that with a cold bench the lawyer has a large measure of control over the court's impressions and the issues that will be discussed. Because oral argument creates a special rapport that cannot be gained from reading briefs, these first impressions are likely to be lasting ones that the court will take with it when it goes into conference to consider the case.

The cold bench has, however, one glaring disadvantage. As a general rule the case is assigned to one judge to read the briefs and record, to report to his colleagues, and to write the opinion. His colleagues have comparable responsibilities with respect to other cases. Consequently the assigned judge tends to feel he "owns" the case; his voice is controlling because his colleagues are uninterested or even bored, and the decision does not represent the best of the court's collective thinking.

The situation is quite different with the hot bench, as I see it, because the court has studied the briefs. It knows both the facts and the legal issues and has had an opportunity to think about them. Most important, the first impression, which is often the most lasting, has already been made by your briefs. Thus, with a hot bench there is a premium on the statement of the facts in your brief, for at the oral argument the hot bench may take the view that it knows the facts and deny you another opportunity to discuss them. Reading the briefs tends to have much the same effect as discovery procedures at the trial level: the issues, both factual and legal, are narrowed, and some of the initiative of the argument passes to the court.

For the advocate, this is both a burden and a blessing. It is a burden, first, because it is almost impossible to prepare the well-organized, flowing argument that you think you would like to make. Remember, you must be flexible, and this you cannot be if you insist on steadfast adherence to a written text. It is a burden, second, because the court's ideas about what are the important issues of fact and law may be erroneous or unfavorable, or both. On occasion, the court will become concerned with issues that you think subsidiary or unimportant. In either case, precious time will be consumed in attempting to dispel these ideas or to correct the erroneous impressions. You may find yourself in the position of having made none of the affirmative argument you had planned.

On the other hand, the hot bench is a blessing because you are given an opportunity to see which of the issues the court thinks most important and what aspects of those issues it finds troublesome. One observer has described appeals in British courts, where cases are often read to the court and discussed in detail during argument, as resembling conversations between gentlemen on a subject of mutual interest. The hot-bench argument in this country has some of the same characteristics: you are discussing subjects that interest the court.

These two characteristics of the hot bench, the need to dispel previous impressions and the opportunity to discuss issues that are troubling the court, ought to be seized upon by counsel. Oral arguments before a hot bench should be flexible enough to take advantage of the fact that the court, by its questions, itself lays the foundation for an argument tailored to meet the very things it finds important or troublesome.

The hot bench also has what I conceive to be an inherent weakness. Since the members of the court have read and discussed the briefs before oral argument, there is a tendency for the entire panel to arrive at a composite judgment —if you will, to freeze—on the ultimate decision even before hearing the oral argument.

I must digress, for a moment, to discuss what I choose to call the "tepid," or "lukewarm," bench. That's the bench on which one or more of the panel try to read the briefs or are engaged in conversation with a colleague while the argument is being presented. The judges cannot concentrate on either the brief or the oral argument. You can only hope that the chandelier will fall and fix their attention on at least one thing and that their consciences will so prick them that later, in the quiet of their chambers, they will apply themselves to a study of the briefs without distraction.

Or, you can follow the example of one of the better-qualified senior appellate lawyers of this city. Some years ago he was making an argument when, almost immediately after he had addressed the court, the three judges huddled in conversation. After a few sentences, the lawyer stopped, hoping his silence would provoke the bench's attention. He succeeded to the extent of being told by the chief judge to proceed. He resumed his argument, and the three judges resumed their huddle. For the second time, the advocate stopped. Again, the conversation among the judges ceased, and the presiding judge said, "I thought I told you to proceed." The lawyer began a third time, and when the judges once more went into their huddle, he loudly closed his notebook, banging it on the podium. Naturally, the judges were startled, and the chief judge inquired, "Is anything wrong?" The lawyer hesitated briefly and then, in a low, dignified voice, said, "Your Honors, I quite understand my position here. I'm a paid advocate, paid to stand here and plead my client's cause. But you are paid to sit there and listen to me." I suggest that such a dramatic gesture should be undertaken only if you have white hair. Even then, as happened to my senior, you probably must content yourself with an adverse decision.

With all respect, I believe such conduct by a panel is a discourtesy to the advocate who has labored hard and long to narrow the issues and to present a helpful argument. More, it is a reflection on the panel itself. Fortunately, in my experience, there are few tepid benches. But enough on this digression. From the standpoint of the appellate lawyers, what are the practical consequences of these differences between the hot and cold benches?

Basically, you must keep in mind the purpose of the appellate process. Reflecting perhaps the difference in perspective, a judge has described that purpose as "the correction of errors" while an advocate has described it as the winning of a "particular case before a particular tribunal for a particular client." Both views are correct, but I think the latter more useful and important for the appellate advocate.

Next, you should find out whether the court before which you are arguing makes a practice of reading the briefs before oral argument, and sometimes this is difficult. Judge Prettyman of the Court of Appeals for the District of Columbia has long urged that courts should announce their practice in this respect. While I am sure that this suggestion would have the unanimous backing of the appellate bar, it has not been adopted. To my knowledge, only the First Department of the Appellate Division here in New York, the New Jersey appellate courts, and the Third Circuit have an openly publicized policy, which is to read the briefs before argument.

Nevertheless, by inquiry it is usually possible to ascertain a court's general practice in this regard. It is my under-

standing that a majority of the members of the New York
Court of Appeals generally do not read the briefs prior to
argument, although some of the judges do. On the other
hand, in most of the United States Courts of Appeal, it is
now the general practice for judges to read the briefs before argument, at least to the point of familiarizing themselves with the issues raised by the appeal. (But of course,
this general familiarization may not suffice to make the
bench hot. There is an old proverb: "A little learning is a
dangerous thing.") The best source of information is to
take a day off and attend a session of the court several days
before your argument is scheduled. See for yourself what
the practice is and how the judges react.

While I emphasize the importance of ascertaining the
usual practice of the court, let me add two caveats. First,
preparation of your oral argument will be much the same
whether you argue before a hot or a cold bench. What you
actually say at the time of the argument will depend
largely on the questions from the bench or, in the case
of the respondent-appellee, on what the appellant's counsel may have said. In either case, you must be thoroughly
prepared. Second, no matter what the court's practice,
never assume that the court is familiar with the case unless
you have been so told by the court itself.

The process of finding out whether you will be arguing
before a relatively hot bench, that is, whether the court
has dealt with similar issues in the past, is usually a matter of simple legal research. You should explore decisions
in related and similar legal areas and then check your generalized conclusions against the opinion of those who have
had some experience with the court. Professor Llewellyn

recommends you read the last volume of the reported cases to get a feel for how the court is reacting. If your search of the cases reveals that the court is sensitive to what might be described as human problems rather than abstract rules of law or if you find that the court is reluctant or unwilling to make new law, then certainly you should verify these conclusions with members of the bar who are better acquainted with the court, for the accuracy of such conclusions may make the difference between winning and losing your case.

The preparation of your appellate argument requires a number of steps. Initially, you face the choice of the issues which you will take up on appeal. In doing so, it is well to remember, as my friend Whitman Knapp has pointed out, that every appellate argument is composed of two elements, intellectual and emotional. This dichotomy arises from the fact that in many, if not most, appeals a plausible judicial opinion could be written to come out on either side of the case. But this does not mean that the just or right decision can go either way. It is your job first to convince the judges that the case ought to be decided in your favor (that is the emotional element) and then to guide them to the proper result by outlining the principles on which they can predicate their decision (the intellectual element).

In choosing the issues that you plan to argue, be selective. In every case there is usually one cardinal issue, and your argument should be directed principally to that issue. As Mr. Davis put it, "Go for the jugular vein." Of course, you may find that your strongest legal issue is a dry point of procedure or evidence with no emotional appeal while only inclusion of a legally weaker issue will bring forward the injustice that has been worked on your client. In such a case and if you have no issue that is strong in both elements, you probably should advance on both fronts in order to bring a full picture to the court, leaving to the court the option of choosing one or both of the legal pegs on which to hang its decision.

Having chosen your issues, you must frame them. This is extremely important. The objective should be so to frame the issues that if your framing is accepted, the decision will be your way. More than that, since your adversary will also be framing the issues as he sees them, yours must be so stated as to become an essential element in the court's view of the case. Professor Llewellyn, who has written and talked a great deal about this matter of issue framing and issue "capture," as he called it, once gave an illustration drawn from the New Testament. As Professor Llewellyn told it in his inimitable fashion, Jesus was in something of a jam. There was a nationalist revolt against a foreign colonial power, and Jesus was representing not the nationalist leaders but a lot of people from the other side of the tracks. He was attracting such a large following that it threatened the power of the nationalist leaders. So they sent around some people to frame Jesus, and when they got Him in the middle of a big crowd, they asked, "Is it lawful to pay tribute unto Caesar?" They thought they had Jesus with one of those "Have you quit beating your wife?" questions. If He said "Yes," then all the nationalists, even those He was leading, would be down on Him, and if He said "No," then the Emperor's police would throw Him in the clink. You remember what Jesus did. He asked for a coin. Then He asked, "Whose is the head and what is the name?" He had posed the issue, and there could only be one answer: "Caesar." Then Jesus followed up by saying, "Render unto Caesar that which is Caesar's and unto God that which is God's."

In framing your issues you must always consider the temper of the court before which you are going to argue. In light of past decisions, should you emphasize facts or law? Should you try to bring your case within existing principles that the court has accepted, or should you attempt to make some new law in a direction in which the court seems to be moving? If you are the appellant, you should ordinarily attempt to bring the issues within the framework of concepts that have already been accepted by the court. Here again, Professor Llewellyn has given us a useful illustration.

A fellow put together a combine between a French syndicate and an American group, operating under the well-established principle of French law that such a person can collect a commission from both sides. The French syndicate paid him, but the Americans thought one commission was enough. He sued in the United States, and the issue turned on whether, being an agent, he had not gotten his commission from his principal. His counsel took the position that since all the facts had been disclosed, the principle of double agency applied: the plaintiff was a double agent and therefore entitled to the double commission. Professor Llewellyn characterized this as "idiotic," because the concept of agency to the ordinary American judge connotes loyalty and diligence and it is fundamental in this country that such fealty cannot be paid to two parties trying to get together on the same deal, since they have conflicting interests. He suggested that the facts—full disclosure and bringing the parties together to make a deal —were such that had the issue been posed in terms of brokerage, carrying no connotations of loyalty and diligence, the case might well have been decided differently, and I am disposed to agree.

In framing the issues, I think it makes little difference whether you ultimately appear before a hot or a cold bench. It is almost inevitable that you will have some opportunity to pose the issues in your own terms, whether as part of your prepared argument or in answer to some question. It is a weapon that you cannot afford to leave in your office.

Now to the argument itself. It is elementary that at the beginning of the argument before a cold bench the court knows little or nothing about your case. This imposes on you the duty of communicating your case with clarity and simplicity. Your opening statement is especially important, for it will set the tone for the whole argument. In addition to describing the nature and the history of the case, you should so pose the basic issue that it will be accepted and will capture the court. A good example of this technique arose out of a case involving the crash of a Brazilian airliner while on a domestic flight in Brazil. The plaintiff, an American residing in New York, sued the airline here and argued that New York law should be applied. The lower court held that Brazilian law was applicable. On appeal, counsel for the appellee airline posed the issue as follows: "Should the plaintiff be given a preferred status over other passengers on the flight from Rio to São Paulo, solely because he is a resident of New York?" The answer was contained in the question as posed.

In making your statement of facts, always keep in mind the three "C's," chronology, candor, and clarity. Begin at the beginning and trace the facts as they developed. Be objective lest your adversary point out an obvious omission. Never be guilty of misleading the court. Simplicity is an absolute essential; avoid details, and if dates or figures are involved, use only years and round numbers unless exactness is critical to the case. The ear can take in only so much, and the brain will retain only part of that. If a court is submerged in details, it will remember next to nothing and the value of the oral argument will be lost. Most important, you must make the facts live for the court. Goethe might have been speaking of many members of our bar when he wrote:

> "He has the pieces in his hand:
>   there fails, alas! only the
>   life-giving bond.

If your statement of the facts contains "the life-giving bond," it will be difficult for your adversary to dispel the impressions you have created.

If you are the respondent-appellee, it will be the rare case when you can with safety accept the appellant's statement of either the facts or the issues. It is easy enough to restate the issues, but be assured that no court likes to hear a new statement of the facts in their entirety. Even if it permits a restatement, the court will find it difficult to mask its annoyance. Confine yourself to the essential points of difference. Even better, if your adversary has been guilty of serious errors, correct him by citations to the record, thereby indirectly discrediting his entire statement.

The appellant's argument on the law should follow much the same pattern as that employed in stating the facts. Clarity, candor, and simplicity are of the essence. One unfortunate consequence of our present system of legal education is that young lawyers find ingenious arguments especially appealing. But these are poison in most appellate courts. A judge approaches an argument that appears to be ingenious with instinctive suspicion; it gives the distinct impression of being merely verbal. If the legal argument appears to flow naturally from well-settled legal principles, you have satisfied in the best possible way the intellectual element of your appeal.

Similarly, the citation of authorities should be kept to a minimum. If the court does not appear to be generally familiar with those cases you believe controlling, limit your argument to a brief summarization of the holding and make specific reference to those pages of your brief that develop the argument in detail. Above all, do not read long quotations. Content yourself with a paraphrase or a pithy quotation of one or two lines.

Of course, if the court is not familiar with the cases referred to by the appellant, the task of the respondent-appellee in attempting to show that they do not stand for the proposition urged by the appellant or that they are to be distinguished from the case at bar is almost impossible. In the time available, one simply cannot argue the meaning of cases the court has not read. Rather, the argument should be limited to casting such doubt on the appellant's interpretation of the cases as will stimulate the court to read the cases. Indeed, in such a situation, that is about all you can do.

Much of what I have just said is also applicable to hot-bench arguments, but with somewhat different effect. You are faced at the outset with the difficulty of organizing an argument to be presented to a court that has already developed notions about the case that have not been divulged to you. The appellant must be far more cautious with his initial statement of the case than with a cold bench, for the court will have already formed some impression of it. Certainly, your statement of the issues cannot be at variance with the statement in your brief, even though your statement may be at variance with the issues the court itself has developed. Similarly, the statement of facts must, in general, be consistent with those recited in the briefs. Otherwise, you are likely to irritate the court, you expose yourself to what may be irrelevant questions, and you may cast doubt on your own integrity.

Before a hot bench, if it's really hot, you may not even have the chance to state either the issues or the facts. You may get as far as saying "May it please the court," only to be reminded that the court has read the record and the briefs, that it does not want to hear anything about the facts, but that it has some questions. And your allotted time may be devoted exclusively to answering questions.

Or, you may be placed in the position of one of my friends who recently appeared before the Appellate Division in a tax case, similar in all respects to one he had argued and won some years previously. He began to state the facts to show the similarity, only to be interrupted by a statement that the court had read the briefs, that it didn't want to hear the facts, and that it wondered if his case wasn't foreclosed by a recent Supreme Court decision. My

friend confesses that before long he was hotter than the
bench, so hot in fact that he never got to the real issue, nor
did he discover that what really bothered the court was
what it mistakenly considered some inconsistency in his position.

This serves to illustrate two things: first, the keynote for
arguing before a hot bench is flexibility; second, that which
we all know—don't get heated yourself. Lawyers too often
ignore the fact that a hot-bench oral argument partakes of
the nature of a conference between court and counsel, and
they resent extensive questioning from the court as an in-
terference with their orderly presentation of the argument.
But if your brief has been properly prepared, the court has
already been subjected to an orderly presentation of the argument. Ideally, at the argument, you want to be able to
induce the court to tell you, albeit in the form of questions,
something about its view of the case. Only in this way can
you take advantage of the opportunity to dispel erroneous
or unfavorable impressions and to answer questions that
are troubling the court. This assumes, of course, that the
court's questions will reveal its problems. Sometimes the
questions seem very obtuse, perhaps because the court
wants to avoid giving the impression that it has prejudged
the case on the merits. I suppose also that in other cases
the judges, like the rest of us, may be guilty of fuzzy thinking.

For this reason counsel for both the appellant and the
respondent-appellee must be fully prepared to jettison their
prepared arguments without notice. In your preparation you
should attempt to discover and uncover, through analysis
of your opponent's brief and discussions with colleagues, all

the questions that are likely to be asked. Your familiarity with the record must be even more intimate than in a cold-bench argument. And you must be prepared to reorganize your argument around the questions of the court.

Let me illustrate, if I may, by a personal reference. I recall a case several years ago before the First Department. The calendar was crowded, and if all the lawyers used the time requested, the court would have sat until almost midnight. My adversary had asked for one hour, and I requested thirty minutes. The appellant had spoken for perhaps two minutes when he fell victim to a barrage of questions. He fended them well, but after about forty minutes both the court and he ran out of ammunition or energy, or maybe both. I confess that I had worked hard on my argument, I had followed all the rules, I had timed it, and I had practiced it before my wife and before the mirror. On the spur of the moment, I figuratively threw my argument in the wastebasket and began by addressing myself briefly to a couple of questions that seemed to be troubling the court and that in one form or another had been asked of appellant's counsel about half a dozen times but never really answered. After answering the questions, I paused, expecting to be given equal treatment with another salvo of questions. Instead, I received a courteous "Thank you," a nice way of saying the court had heard enough from me. Not until several weeks later did I learn that my opponent's answers had not convinced the court of the rightness of his client's cause.

The foregoing, I think, illustrates one point. Just as the cold-bench argument gives some advantage to the appellant because he has the first crack at the court, so a hot-bench argument gives some advantage to the respondent-appellee. It may be difficult for the appellant to determine the issues that really concern the court until he is well into his argument or has been asked a series of questions. But the respondent-appellee has the advantage of having heard all the questions that have been put to the appellant and can frame his argument around answering those questions in a way favorable to his client.

In his speech on oral advocacy, John W. Davis set forth ten basic rules. The last of those commandments was "Sit down." I think that I have come to the point in this discussion when that commandment must be obeyed.

QUESTION PERIOD

QUESTION: Mr. Gates, if you are before a cold bench with a complicated record and in an area of law that is both difficult and unfamiliar to the court, what can you do?

MR. GATES: In such a situation, you are faced with a difficult problem, but I shall do my best to answer.

I shall repeat what I said a little bit earlier. I do not think that in appellate argument you should get into the details of the facts. You have to treat the factual situation with a broad brush, emphasizing only those details that are critical to your particular case.

More often than not, there is only one cardinal legal issue, even in the circumstance that you have described. I would spend 90 percent of my time making sure that the court had a real feel for the facts and 10 percent of my time on the legal issue and hope that the court would thereafter read my brief that did discuss in detail the complete legal issues.

QUESTION: Would the hotness or the coldness of the bench affect significantly the way in which you organized your brief, and if so, how?

MR. GATES: Not significantly, but I am sure that if my bench is hot, I take great pains with the statement of facts and of the issues. I believe them to be of paramount importance because the impression that the court gets from reading your brief is an impression that is carried forward into the oral argument and stimulates its questioning. It is desirable that that impression should be the correct one so that you don't have to dissipate your time in oral argument coping with ideas that the judges may have developed on their own.

My colleague Mr. Pollack tells of an experience that he had recently. It was a case before a hot bench, and the appellant's brief was very badly prepared. The court couldn't understand what the man was driving at in the brief. When he got up to make his argument, the judges couldn't understand what he was trying to say. I submit to you that had the brief been properly prepared, the questions directed from the court might well have solved the problem with respect to his oral argument.

QUESTION: Mr. Gates, do you believe in the technique of a very carefully phrased opening sentence on an argument, perhaps one that is written out right in front of you?

MR. GATES: I certainly do. I will make a confession. Although I spoke from notes tonight, I wrote the speech before I made the notes from which I spoke.

I always believe it is essential that your opening should be so well ingrained in your mind that no matter what happens you get started on the right foot, particularly if you are representing an appellant. Something may happen, particularly if you are an appellee or respondent, that will cause you to change your opening, but you have got it there so you can use it if it is opportune.

QUESTION: Mr. Gates, what is your experience in handling an appeal when you have the problem of no oral argument? How do you handle your brief? Do you handle it any differently from the way you do when you are going to have one?

MR. GATES: Your brief and your statement of facts must carry the whole burden of persuasion, but I don't think they should be greatly different from those written for cases with oral argument.

QUESTION: Suppose a hot bench raises a question that you have not anticipated or that you feel is somewhat off the point, or suppose you are quite sure there is an answer to it but you don't have the authority at your fingertips. I have read in textbooks that what you should do is request leave to file a supplemental brief. Against that I would balance, from experience perhaps, the almost sure conviction that a supplemental brief, if you do file it, is not going to be read or will be read very quickly. How are you able in the heat of the argument to make an intelligent judgment as to when to take a calculated risk to try and deal with the thing on your feet and when to say, "I just don't know enough, and I want to have a chance to look it up"?

MR. GATES: I think we all have to recognize our limitations. No matter how thoroughly you prepare, there always is the possibility that the court will focus on some point that you may not have seen at all or have chosen to believe was unimportant.

I believe humility is a great thing, and if I feel I am not really able to cope with the problem, I have no reluctance to say, "May it please the court, I should like to file a supplemental brief on this subject." I believe that if the court presses you to the point at which you feel you must offer to file a supplemental brief, the judges are really interested in the question and that you don't have to worry about their reading the brief after it is filed.

QUESTION: There is a theory that if you have a weakness in your case or some trouble, some point that should be answered, and that if the court does not raise it in oral argument, you should see that by the time you finish your argument you have answered this question so the court will not raise it in conference when you don't have a chance to present your view. How would you apply this theory to a hot bench and a cold bench?

MR. GATES: In the case of the hot bench, you can be pretty sanguine that the court will ask you something about that point. If it doesn't, then I think it is a pretty good idea to make mention of it somewhere in the argument, perhaps to stimulate the court to ask questions so you have a complete opportunity to present what you think to be the strongest arguments in your favor on the point.

QUESTION: I take it that for a cold bench you would raise the point some time early in your argument.

MR. GATES: Certainly.

QUESTION: I take it that on arguing the law you advise that counsel not get bogged down in details but merely express to the court the general principles of law that are applicable.

MR. GATES: I would go somewhat further than that. I would give the holding of particular pertinent cases but not get into detailed discussion of any one case unless I were asked by the court to make distinctions. But, of course, there are exceptions to a general rule.

QUESTION: That is what I was getting at. I was assuming that the court knew the general law and that the appellant lawyer was really there to push the esoteric case or the exceptional principles. That requires, does it not, getting into detail; otherwise you don't get the attention of the court.

MR. GATES: You can't answer that in generalities. If you have a case, for example (and I am going to switch just a little bit), in which you get into legislative history because that is important to the interpretation of a statute, you may have to go back to legislative records and trace the legislation, step by step, to show the legislative intention.

So it is with some arguments involving past decisions. However, I do suggest to you that, at least in my experience, you waste your time in trying to differentiate the fine points of three or four different cases to show why they don't apply here or why they do apply there. I don't think the court moves that fast.

References Made by Mr. Gates

Davis, John W., *The Argument of an Appeal,* 26 ABAJ 895 (1940). Wiener, Frederick Bernays, *Briefing and Arguing Federal Appeals,* Bureau of National Affairs, Washington, D.C., 1961.

The Federal Appeal

THURGOOD MARSHALL

Mr. Justice Marshall, who became a member of the United States Supreme Court on September 1, 1967, formerly served as Solicitor General of the United States and as judge of the United States Court of Appeals for the Second Circuit. He took his legal training at Howard University. He was active in the advocacy of civil-rights cases while serving as special counsel for the NAACP.

As you can tell from what the previous speakers in this series have said, there is no one particular way of being an effective advocate, and each of us finds this out each time he appears in court. Some of you have argued as many cases as I have, if not more; therefore, I won't presume to state anything more than my own views, with no attempt to persuade you of their universal applicability.

Nor will I set forth a list of rules for the effective appellate advocate in the federal courts. Several speakers have alluded to John W. Davis's superb 1940 speech, "The Argument of an Appeal," in which are set forth ten commandments any advocate should observe. In addition, Frederick Bernays Wiener has written an *apologia pro vita sua, Briefing and Arguing Federal Appeals*—which, incidentally, he might easily have called *My Life in Court* —thoroughly covering the subject.

Hence, I think it is safe to assume that every lawyer knows that the prerequisites for effective appellate advocacy are such points as making a concise, sympathetic, yet accurate statement of the facts and phrasing an issue to capture the interest of the court both intellectually and emotionally.

I won't tell you how to win a case on appeal, though of all the answers I have thought of over the years, only one is close to being accurate. Why did I qualify my statement by saying "is close to being accurate"? I cannot forget the case of *Lyons v Oklahoma*. In that murder case, tried in a small town in Oklahoma, my client was convicted and sentenced to life imprisonment.

After the trial, the assistant attorney general of Oklahoma and the trial judge both assured me privately that I would get a reversal on the confession point. After I had lost by 2 to 1 in the Court of Criminal Appeals of Oklahoma, I was again assured privately by the court and the assistant attorney general I would win in the Supreme Court.

By the time the case was argued in the Supreme Court of the United States all sides and everyone else in the world were in complete agreement: I was a sure winner. End of the story: The judgment was affirmed. Perhaps we should have a course entitled "How to Win the Sure Winners." Rather than that, I would pass on to you the answer I give to people who ask, "What is the most important case you have argued?" My reply has always been, "The next one."

A federal appeal, as I shall define it, is any case argued before a federal appellate court, primarily the Courts of Appeals and the Supreme Court. Thus, a state case brought to the Supreme Court is a federal appeal at least for tonight.

It is impossible to draw a clear line between a federal appeal and a state appeal. The jurisdictional boundaries we all know. Once they have been established, the advocacy in handling the particular appeal is much the same. The same is true of the lawyers preparing and arguing the appeals. For example, there is no longer even a small, recognizable Supreme Court bar. The percentage of federal appeals is growing at an accelerated rate, and the number of lawyers handling these appeals is, likewise, increasing daily. Statistics show a similar increase in appeals in state courts. Therefore, I cannot resist the temptation to make a few comments on appellate advocacy in general.

It is particularly important in an appellate court to know the tribunal. As the then Judge Cardozo said, "The great tides and currents which engulf the rest of men do not turn aside in their course and pass judges by."

Most lawyers can't help but know something of the views of the Justices of the Supreme Court and of each individual Justice thereof. But the admonition is just as true of the Courts of Appeals, although there is not nearly as much published material concerning the latter. In the Supreme Court you always know who the members of the panel are, while in some of the Courts of Appeals you discover the members of the panel only when they enter the courtroom —surprise!

I can remember my first sitting in the Court of Appeals for the Second Circuit. I sat with Justices Waterman and Smith, and those of you who know them know that the three of us are of about the same size. When the three of us walked in, one of the lawyers said, "What! The forward line of Notre Dame!"

I would not want you to infer from these remarks that the quality of justice in a Court of Appeals depends on the particular panel assigned to a case. That is far from the truth. However, an effective advocate must not be oblivious to the interests of the particular judges before whom he is arguing.

For example, a judge quite often grows fond of a particular opinion on which he has labored for weeks or months. Would you insult him by not having read his *magnum opus*, published just three days before your argument? Would you expect to discuss poetry with Robert Penn Warren, having read only his novels, or discuss art with Picasso, having seen only the paintings of his early blue period?

Indeed, knowledge of a judge's recent opinions aside, knowing the panel members, their background and interests, provides valuable clues that will enable you to answer questions in a way that will, as the late Karl Llewellyn once said, "capture the court." Of course, a judge wants to do justice, but it is the advocate's job to interest him enough to do so by deciding the case correctly—for your client, obviously.

A word of caution is in order. I do not suggest that the lawyer should pander to what he considers to be the judge's personal intuitions, real or fancied. To the contrary, I urge that you should be aware of the judge's stated views of the law involved and try to convince him that the position you assert is at least encompassed within his overall views. On the other hand, to attempt to play up to any judge's alleged personal views as contrasted with his true legal opinions is to play Russian roulette.

All the lawyers I know, especially those who have written on advocacy, stress the importance of oral argument. Most judges do, too. I suspect that those who don't have become so inured to the poor arguments that are often made that they do not appreciate the value of oral argument in general. During a few arguments in the Second Circuit, I've recalled with approval the remark in *King Henry VI, Part II*, "The first thing we do, let's kill all the lawyers."

We all know that in the Supreme Court and in many of the Courts of Appeals, votes are cast and opinion writing assigned soon after argument, usually within a week. Although those votes may later change, in most cases, I think it accurate to say, they don't. The impression you leave with the judges in the courtroom is often the impression on which they decide your case, but this is based on the prior reading of the brief as well as on the oral argument.

The volume of appeals in federal courts is steadily increasing. The number of appeals in the Courts of Appeals has increased by over 50 percent in the last four years. Too many litigants are taking literally Ambrose Bierce's definition of an appeal: "In law, to put the dice into the box for another throw."

In the last fiscal year, the number of appeals docketed in the Second Circuit, for example, increased by 20 percent. Yet you still have the same amount of time in which to argue your case. If a federal judge has less time to read the briefs and so on, must he not rely more on you personally in the courtroom to point out the key issues, the tentative resolution?

One difficulty with increasing volume is that it causes some judges to go into the courtroom completely cold. In an earlier speech Mr. Gates professed to find some advantages in a cold bench. I suspect he was merely trying to make the best of an existing situation. If a judge hasn't read the briefs, at least to the extent of acquiring familiarity with the facts and knowledge of the issues, then he can't participate with counsel in a fruitful discussion, which is what a good oral argument is.

Recently I heard a Justice of the Supreme Court tell a

group of judges and lawyers that when he was an advocate
he assumed that after he had briefed and argued a case,
the judge had no difficulty in using the brief and argument to write his opinion. He believed that nothing more
was needed. However, when he reached the other side of
the bench, he discovered to his surprise that he had to do
considerable research and work in deciding the case.

Regardless of the panel you get, the questions you get,
or the answers you give, I maintain it is the brief that does
the final job, if for no other reason than that opinions are
often written several weeks and sometimes months after
argument. The arguments, great as they may have been,
are forgotten. In the seclusion of his chambers the judge
has only the briefs and the law books. At that time your
brief is your only spokesman.

I suppose that the distinctive feature of a federal appeal
and one that is of obvious significance to the advocate is
the nature of the issues usually presented. Of course, there
are many federal appeals, in diversity cases for example,
that differ little from the typical appeal in a state court.
However, in a number of federal appeals the issues become
larger than the particular interests represented by the immediate litigants. A question of the interpretation of a
federal statute decided by the Second Circuit has import
far beyond the court's geographical limits. And, of course,
virtually all the cases in the Supreme Court are of national
significance in one way or another, for that is the very nature of Supreme Court litigation.

In the October, 1964, term of the Supreme Court there
were 2,178 applications for review. Only 132 were accepted
for argument. I think it clear that many of those 2,000-

plus applications should not have been submitted to the Court. Thus, the advocate in the Supreme Court and, in many cases, in the Courts of Appeals must be prepared to relate his case to the law generally, to advise the court why the change urged, or the *status quo* to be preserved, is desirable, and to inform the court of the consequences of the position he advocates, because the court is looking beyond the interests of the parties immediately before it.

Did anyone doubt that the positions of the parties in *Brown v Board of Education* portended the demise of more than just segregated schools? What about *Gideon, Mapp,* and *Escobedo*? When the Supreme Court asked if *Betts v Brady* should be reconsidered, wasn't it clear that the Court was concerned with more than just the fate of Clarence Gideon?

In noting that, as a matter of national scope, issues in federal appeals are more likely to transcend the immediate case, I should state that it is frequently the advocate's most interesting and difficult task to convince the Supreme Court to take his case on certiorari. At the same time, all too many lawyers feel that petitioning for certiorari, regardless of the objective significance of the case, is as necessary as noting an appeal to the Court of Appeals, thus burdening the Supreme Court.

With regard to grounds for appeal to the Courts of Appeals and for petitioning to the United States Supreme Court, I think often of the lawyer whose only complaint is not yet a recognized ground for appeal or certiorari, to wit, "I am unhappy with the lower court's decision." You have got to have more.

There are many cases decided adversely to the government that the Solicitor General decides not to take to the Supreme Court because he feels that the case is not "cert-worthy." Because of that exercise of judgment, naturally, a greater percentage of government petitions are granted.

While it is true that government cases often present significant and recurring issues of the kind calling for Supreme Court review, there is still room for the skill of an effective advocate in the borderline cases.

For example, *United States v Ventresca* did not present an issue of great importance. The issue was whether or not an affidavit in support of a search warrant was sufficient to establish probable cause.

Indeed, the government's petition began: "The Solicitor General seeks certiorari in this small and intrinsically unimportant case. . . ." We felt that the Court of Appeals had read the particular affidavit in an unduly technical manner. We sought certiorari in the belief that—

> upholding the activities of law-enforcement agencies that have scrupulously observed the procedure for safeguarding constitutional rights and satisfying the substantial requirements for a search warrant is no less important than the invalidation of convictions because of disregard for individual rights or official overreaching.

Our petition was granted, and we prevailed on the Court, with the majority opinion stating 380 US at 111–112:

> This court is alert to invalidate unconstitutional searches and seizures whether with or without a warrant. . . . By doing so, it vindicates individual liberties and strengthens the administration of justice by promoting respect for law and order. This Court is equally concerned to uphold the actions of law enforcement officers consistently following the proper constitutional course. This is no less important

to the administration of justice than the invalidation of convictions because of disregard of individual rights or official overreaching.

I think the *Ventresca* case is a good example of the role played by an effective advocate. Of course, we can all think of other examples.

Supreme Court practice requires three distinct types of presentation. The petition for certiorari must be short, concise, and exemplary of John W. Davis's admonition, "Go for the jugular vein." The decision of the lower court is not only clearly wrong, it is shocking and, if allowed to stand, will disrupt the entire existing federal judicial system. It is not only worthy of review, but it is, likewise, of compelling national significance. The country simply couldn't exist without the review.

Now, if by any chance certiorari is granted, the brief on the merits must prove that point. There is where you get the problem, and it's a problem that grows. If certiorari is granted without any limitation, you are confronted with the question of which subsidiary point to brief and of how much briefing is to be done on that point and how much on the other points. How far must you go into legislative history on a minor point?

One thing is certain. You cannot approach a brief on the merits without a well-organized plan and careful appraisal. The rules themselves clearly point to the proper procedure.

Once you have carefully prepared an adequate statement of the case and a concise and convincing summary of argument, your outline should be complete. You should have the answer to the question presented. Little advice can be given on the final problem: to be short and concise without losing either a point or the flavor of a point. The solution, of course, must vary with the case and with the draftsman. It could very well be true that some briefs are too long, and, indeed, I am a witness to it. There was a brief in the school cases, the brief on the merits. It totaled 250-odd pages. The one thing I remember about that brief was that during the final printing, late one Sunday night, the printer called us and said he thought a change would have to be made on the cover. We asked what should be changed, and he said, "Very frankly, do you really want to call this book a brief?"

The final step, of course, is oral argument. Here my admonition would be that in preparing for the argument you make every effort to escape the inevitable, that is, that the best answer any of us has made to a question or questions from the bench is the one he thinks of in the cab on the way back to the hotel from the court.

You should bear that in mind in preparing your argument, and canvass thoroughly the points that are obvious and inherent in the questions. Be prepared for more questions than you get, and be sure your answers are accurate and concise and are prepared with complete candor. Nonresponsive and evasive answers merely invite the guillotine.

Finally, on this point, be sure you understand the question and its implications. Often when you hear the start of a question and it appears to be just the one you have been waiting for, you miss the rest of the question, which is what the justice is interested in. Your answer is less than satisfactory, and you give the impression of being evasive.

Much of what has been suggested for the Supreme Court,

of course, is equally applicable to an appeal in the Court of Appeals. Although the federal judiciary consists of courts of limited jurisdiction, the issues run from constitutional questions to those of less widespread importance presented in, for example, diversity automobile cases.

I have always been impressed, astonished—you pick the word—when not only in brief after brief but in opinion after opinion you see sentence after sentence saying this: "Our diversity case is controlled by *Erie v Tompkins*, citation so-and-so and so-and-so." For the life of me, why in this day and age you need the citation of *Erie v Tompkins* eludes me, but it still appears.

While little specialized assistance is needed in the appeal of a diversity case, a word should be given on appeals and other actions that review actions or rulings of federal administrative agencies. There are the restrictions beginning with the *Universal Camera* case and later refinements of that rule.

The substantial-evidence rule is meant to be restrictive in the presentation and decision of administrative agency appeals. At the same time, it is not a control of the intensity of judicial review. The scope of review may be broad or narrow and still comply with the substantial-evidence rule. It depends on the court. A clear expression of the true rule is set out by Professor Davis in his *Administrative Law Treatise*:

> The scope of review of findings of a judge without a jury, however, is different from the scope of review of administrative findings and of jury verdicts, for findings of a judge may be upset if they are clearly erroneous. Be-

cause findings may be clearly erroneous without being un-reasonable so as to be upset under the substantial-evidence rule, the scope of review of administrative findings is nar-rower than the scope of review of a judge's findings.

In the briefing and arguing of the administrative appeal, this problem is intensified by the inevitable long and com-plex record inherent in all governmental-agency hearings. After all, the lawyers are paid by the day! Inevitably there are tens or hundreds of what appear to be errors and lack of what is considered to be sufficiently substantial evidence. The temptation is to brief and argue each of the points. Better practice is to pick the big ones and hammer home on them. Be certain, however, that the points are big enough to do the job.

I should also mention one other problem, which is habeas corpus—all those petitions for review of sentences long since passed. My only answer is that there is little that anyone can give in a short talk like this to cover them. I point the petitions out merely to compliment the bar and especially the bar of the Second Circuit for the large number of voluntary lawyers who have come forth in this very difficult field to give these men the rep-resentation that the law requires them to have.

I have not put emphasis in this talk on the appellee, or respondent, the bottom side of these cases, because practi-cally all I have said applies to whichever side you are on. The only thing I do want to mention is that I am more and more impressed by the failure of lawyers to use a beautiful opinion by the lower court, scholarly done, bust-ing with research. It is sad to see an appellee or respondent prepare his brief, finish his oral argument, and never once rely on the opinion of the judge below.

I mention that merely as one addition. Finally, I close with the frustration I started with. Having gone over the books and articles on federal appellate procedures and having prepared these few remarks and done the best I can, I still have the feeling that I should end as I started, with John W. Davis's "Go for the jugular vein." There is not one of you in this room who hasn't read it at some time or another. Hardly 1 out of 100 lawyers has filed a case on appeal who is not familiar with that admonition—go for the jugular vein—but when you hear the arguments and read the briefs of so many of those lawyers, you find that in aiming for the jugular vein they have put a pinprick in a small vein of the big toe.

QUESTION PERIOD

QUESTION: Why doesn't the Supreme Court get additional judges, a second panel like that of the Second Circuit? Isn't it a fact that certiorari necessarily must be denied in worthy cases because of the heavy case load that the Court has? Why doesn't it get sufficient personnel to handle these many certiorari applications that are worthwhile and should be considered more seriously?

MR. MARSHALL: In my own view, the majority of the petitions for certiorari are of such an unimportant caliber that I don't believe you need another court or more judges. You should see some of the petitions.

You must realize that the Courts of Appeals do a good job. They are the courts where the work is really done, and in a well-presented and fought-out case they tend to arrive at a reasonable answer to the questions presented. If you proliferate Supreme Courts, you proliferate Courts of Appeals, and we shall have more appellate courts than we have trial courts.

I know of one case, a criminal case with a direct appeal to the Court of Appeals, in which a pauper insisted that we give him a lawyer. We gave him a lawyer, a very good one, and the lawyer could find nothing wrong with the record. I know you won't agree that that is ever possible in a criminal trial, but take my word, please, that there was no error in this one.

The lawyer went to his client, who insisted that the lawyer appeal on the point that it was a reversible error for the judge in a three-count indictment, guilty on all three counts, to sentence him on count two before he sentenced him on count one. You would be surprised at the number of cases like that that go to Supreme Court.

My answer is: I think the Supreme Court is capable of handling the cases that come up there. You wouldn't get a better break if you had more judges.

QUESTION: I think I found myself in disagreement on your suggestion that the lawyer address himself to the particular judge's previous opinions. It seems to me it detracts somewhat from your emphasis on the jugular vein in the instant case if you start worrying about previous opinions of the judge instead of trying to direct his attention to what you are actually doing here.

MR. MARSHALL: What are you going to do if you can come within the previous opinion of Judge X only by giving up some of your minor points?

QUESTION: Is this previous opinion directly concerned with the case you are dealing with?

MR. MARSHALL: Pretty closely. I shall give you an example. In the United States Supreme Court, some Justices have made it clear by their opinions that they believe that it is good if Congress operates under Section 5 of the Fourteenth Amendment but that the Court shouldn't expand the Fourteenth Amendment on its own.

You are arguing a case by urging the validity of an act of Congress admittedly adopted under Section 5. The Justice asks you, "Do you want me to agree with you that the Court can extend the Fourteenth Amendment?" "Oh, no," is your answer, "I am arguing that Congress can do it."

That is what I am talking about. If you are in the same substantive field, as you digest opinions over a period of time, it becomes obvious that Judge X's view of the law is thus and so. If you can bring your case within his view ethically and honestly, do it. But don't prostitute yourself.

QUESTION: I have read somewhere that judges object to oral argument that rehashes the brief or that is mainly a restatement of the brief. Where do you draw the line on what you argue and what you brief?

MR. MARSHALL: Well, I don't know of a single judge who doesn't strenuously object to the rehashing of a brief. The judge has read the brief. Once you have prepared your brief, use your argument to prepare yourself for the questions. It is not what is in your brief. I have seen instances in which rehashing has been tried. I have seen instances in which it has been done. I have seen no instances in which it has worked.

Along the same line, waste not too much time on facts. There are very few cases in which facts are important unless they are tied up with the law. Get to the point as soon as you can, not following the brief but your own analysis of what the real issue is. You have to make three different presentations of the same point. That is what makes a good advocate. In all of these you have to be a little Madison Avenue. You have to work the issue around so it is presentable, palatable, and what the court wants.

QUESTION: I should like to ask about the respondent's obligation of candor to the Court with respect to these two problems: (1) How does the government decide when to confess error? (2) If the Supreme Court grants certiorari on a limited question, what do you do with the other points of the case on which you are weak?

MR. MARSHALL: Let me take the first problem: how we confess error.

My first opportunity to confess error was a very simple one. It was in an obscenity case. It seems that Mr. and Mrs. X, husband and wife, legally married, had taken pictures of each other in the nude and had mailed them in a sealed envelope across state lines. The pictures were developed and mailed back in a sealed envelope, and the local United States attorney decided that had interfered with the king's peace.

He prosecuted; both were convicted. The judge gave the man nine months and the wife six months. The Court of Appeals affirmed the conviction. The case got to me. I filed a memorandum with the Supreme Court in which I said that it was against the public policy of the United States to prosecute such cases, even though technically there was a violation of law.

I urged the Supreme Court to send the case back to the District Court with instructions to dismiss it and turn the people loose. I got considerable flak about it. The justices wanted to know what I meant by the public policy of the United States. I said, "That's me."

Since these pictures never reached anybody, nobody saw them. I don't think a man should go to jail for the sole reason that he is stupid. After all, he could have used a Polaroid camera.

It is my understanding—and I have done a little study, naturally, about how often the government does it and when to do it—that we very seldom confess error. It is pretty hard to do. You have got to be pretty sure of the ground. I remember that a predecessor of mine confessed error and that the Supreme Court refused to accept the confession, ordered that the case be argued, and ruled with the government. That predecessor is still trying to figure out whether that was a win or a loss. You have a real problem in confessing error. I don't think it is too important.

What was the other problem you had?

VOICE: If certiorari is granted on a limited question.

MR. MARSHALL: That, I think, is another problem we are debating right now. We have got it on two cases. I know of instances in which the Supreme Court has granted certiorari on point A and decided on point X. You know of those cases.

What do you do? Do you throw away everything but A? I would say that if you are convinced that you have got points B, C, and D, the smartest thing to do is to brief A thoroughly and, near the end, "take in" B and C. Be sure you do this at the end, because when the Justice stops reading, you want to be sure he has thoroughly read point A. That is a real problem.

VOICE: I asked from the other standpoint, from the respondent's standpoint, what you would do if you are weak on B and C and you have been given a way out by the Court because it has granted certiorari only on A.

MR. MARSHALL: I wouldn't touch the other points, normally. This whole thing adds up to a matter of judgment. Even after you have made your judgment, you may feel that you have made a mistake and given away your case, but you still have to make that judgment.

QUESTION: You said the facts are not important. Do you mean only in an appeal to the Supreme Court, or do you mean in any appeal?

MR. MARSHALL: I say that is true in the majority of appeals. If your facts are well briefed and you have limited time, I insist you go to the jugular vein. Don't allow the facts to take up the major part of your time. But there are some instances in which the whole case consists of law involved with facts. Then you spread the whole thing out together, without the simple statement.

QUESTION: In your present position as Solicitor General, what is your feeling about going beyond the record?

MR. MARSHALL: In brief, it is my position that if the Solicitor General, the Attorney General, or the attorney general of any state has facts that he considers important for the Supreme Court's determination of the case and explains where he got them, he can do it. For a private litigant, I am not too sure.

I have seen briefs dating as far back as twenty-odd years in which the Solicitor General or the Attorney General has adopted the practice. The Court expects it from the representative of the government. Indeed, the Justices have been asking recently about some other things that they want us to talk about.

VOICE: To what extent does the Second Circuit go beyond the appendix in the brief to the record itself?

MR. MARSHALL: My experience on the Second Circuit is that at least the writer of the opinion reads the original transcript. There are also several judges of the Court of Appeals who, whether they participate or not, don't limit themselves to the appendix. They read the whole record.

However, if I were you, I would put a point that you want in the appendix and not rely on the judge's reading it elsewhere. That is your job. There are Circuits in which the transcript doesn't even go around. Nothing goes around but the appendix.

QUESTION: Can you really assess the relative impact of an oral argument, particularly in a situation in which the time for writing the opinion is fairly far removed? For example, can the oral argument really make up for a thoroughly rotten brief—something of that sort? How important can the oral argument be?

MR. MARSHALL: I can tell you this. There are a very few occasions when after oral argument the court will decide that one side has got the better of it and yet the judge assigned to write the opinion will later send you a little note saying, "This thing just won't write." Does that give you an idea of how good an oral argument can be?

Now, suppose you make a topflight oral argument, you answer all the questions perfectly, and the three judges say in the courtroom that you have won and that Judge X will write the opinion. Judge X picks up your brief, and the more he reads it, the more he wonders what you are talking about. You are in trouble.

That is why I say that regardless of the oral argument, that last manuscript is speaking for you late at night in the judge's chambers with nobody else there. Even the law clerk has gone home. There is nobody else there but your brief.

QUESTION: Is there any calculated attempt on the Circuits now to affirm in open court rather than take the case back in the chambers and take time on appeal?

MR. MARSHALL: There is a great division among judges on the Courts of Appeals. I am for affirming in open court if the case is clean and clear and if all three of the judges are thoroughly familiar with the record and the briefs. I am for doing it.

There are judges who say that it is not quite right for a poor old lawyer. My answer as an advocate is that, if I am going to lose, I would rather lose right then and there.

Some cases are not worthy of a well-reasoned opinion, and

the circuits have been trying to work out something to circumvent preparing one. Even if you rule from the bench, the client is entitled to a statement of why he lost. I am not entirely sure that the lawyer is entitled to one, because I have a sneaking suspicion he not only knows why he lost but he knew it a considerable time before he lost. But all the judges I have ever talked to think that the client should have a short statement. Whether you should print it or not, I don't know, but on the Second Circuit the rule has been that if a case is decided from the bench, a short statement must be issued within twenty-four hours.

There are some cases that have no present value. One case I decided concerned the verdict of a jury which upheld a woman's claim that in a supermarket in some little town up in Vermont a can of baked beans fell off the shelf and hit her on the shoulder. That is a really earthshaking precedent! I didn't see any reason for it, but we did write the case up.

QUESTION: Would you care to comment on the rule of a full-bench rehearing?

MR. MARSHALL: I have a personal view on that. I am more convinced than when I was on the Second Circuit that the Supreme Court pays no more attention to a 5-to-4 split *en banc* than it would to a 2-to-1 split of a panel. I don't think it influences them at all. It is the issue that is involved. I think a full bench is necessary at times because of the importance of some issues.

As for rehearings in general, I think they are very good. A former chief judge of the Second Circuit used to say he enjoyed reading petitions for rehearings since that was the only time the lawyer could take his hair down and tell the judge what he thought about him, because he had nothing to lose.

References Made by Mr. Marshall

CASES

Betts v Brady (1942) 316 US 455
Brown v Board of Education (1954) 347 US 483
Erie v Tompkins (1938) 304 US 64
Escobedo v Illinois (1964) 378 US 478
Gideon v Wainwright (1963) 372 US 335
Lyons v Oklahoma (1943) 77 Okl Cr 197, 138 P2d 142, 140 P2d 248, 322 US 596
Mapp v Ohio (1961) 367 US 643
United States v Ventresca (1965) 380 US 102
Universal Camera Corp. v NLRB (1951) 340 US 474

OTHER

Davis, John W., *The Argument of an Appeal*, 26 ABAJ 895 (1940).
Davis, Kenneth C., *Administrative Law Treatise*, West, St. Paul, Minn., 1958, at §29.02.
Wiener, Frederick Bernays, *Briefing and Arguing Federal Appeals*, Bureau of National Affairs, Washington, D.C., 1961.

Appellate Courts Compared

SIMON H. RIFKIND

*Simon H. Rifkind, a former judge of the United
States District Court, Southern District of New York
(1941–1950), is a senior partner in the New York
law firm of Paul, Weiss, Rifkind, Weiss and
Garrison. A graduate of the Columbia Law School
and a member of Phi Beta Kappa, he has in his
distinguished career as an advocate and judge
received honorary degrees from Columbia University,
the Jewish Theological Seminary, and Hofstra College.
He has served as chairman of both the Executive
and the Administrative Boards of the American
Jewish Committee and is a member of the American
College of Trial Lawyers and The Association
of the Bar of the City of New York.*

Ladies and gentlemen, you have heard in this room so many splendid addresses about appellate advocacy that I wonder whether there is anything that I can possibly add. My intention is not to give you a lecture about appellate advocacy. You have already absorbed the others and are probably satiated with them; but I thought I would share some gossip with you, some professional small talk about what happens in appellate courtrooms.

My observation has been that many lawyers rather enjoy engaging in that kind of professional gossip. It is all part of the climate in which professionally we live. If you will understand that what I am intending to do is not to deliver a lecture but just to engage in some conversation, you won't be disappointed. Of course, I am the most garrulous party to this conversation, and you will have to wait your turn until the end of my turn.

The title of the subject of tonight's discussion brings to my mind an old vaudeville skit. Some of you are old enough to remember Gallagher and Sheen, and if I remember the skit correctly, it ran something like this:

GALLAGHER: Oh, Mr. Sheen, how is your wife?
SHEEN: Compared to whom, Mr. Gallagher?

"Appellate Courts Compared" is the title of tonight's address. Compared to what? Comparisons, I read somewhere in Shakespeare, are odorous.

Sometimes we evoke a comparison unconsciously. I remember a former justice of the New York Supreme Court, now gone to his reward, who used to walk down to the courthouse wearing a cutaway coat and carrying a cane. When a lawyer would meet him on the avenue and say, "Good morning, how is your Honor?" he would say, "Mine's fine, how is yours?"

Whether comparisons are odious or odorous, there is no question in my mind that they are hazardous. After all, I earn my living by practicing in the very courts I am asked to compare. Judge Breitel, who is very secure in his high place on the bench, apparently attributes a similar sense of security to me, in my lowly place in the well. If so, I take it as a high compliment, but on decision days I sometimes experience a gnawing doubt whether I am warranted in feeling quite that secure. Especially on Thursdays I sometimes acquire what Judge Wallace used to call the Appellate Division blues, those Appellate Division reserved-decision, affirmed-without-opinion blues.

The subject on which I shall discourse with you is, I must confess, a new one to me. Not until Judge Breitel assigned me this task had I ever consciously asked myself whether lawyers in general or I in particular behaved differently in the several appellate courts. Since the assignment, I have both observed and reflected and I have discovered what I should have known long ago. There are indeed differences in the behavior of lawyers in the several appellate courts.

These differences are responsive to a number of significant factors which differentiate one court from another. By way of an anticipatory illustration I suggest, for instance, that you compare an appellate argument before a single judge reviewing, say, a referee's decision in bankruptcy or a report of a special master with an argument before a multi-judge court, say, the Supreme Court of the United States. I think you will agree with me that even though counsel is the same, even though the underlying question is the same, nevertheless there will be a difference in the argument, a difference in rhythm, a change in pace, a variation in pitch. In short, the sound of the music will be different.

I said earlier that in the course of my preparations I observed the behavior of some of my competitors. Let me make a confession to you: that is not an easy thing to do. It is very difficult to observe your competitors in the appellate business. The difficulty springs from the implacability of a rule that I have discovered and that I believe you will confirm me in. That rule is this: In the whole universe of oral discourse, nothing is as boring as the arguments that precede yours on the day's calendar.

No matter how pleasing the architecture of the chamber, no matter how comfortable the upholstered chair, no matter how fine the acoustics or mellifluous the voice, not all of these together overcome the competing circumstance that the notes of your own argument are throbbing in your warm hand, your opening sentence is already formed on your lips, and you are condemned to sit there and listen to a speaker who is wasting precious minutes which manifestly you can put to much more productive use, if only he would make them available to you.

It takes time and effort, my friends, to achieve a reasonable degree of tolerance or resignation. While you are in that state, sometimes, on rare occasions, a miracle happens. You suddenly discover that you are listening. Your attention has been captured. When that occurs, please treasure the moment. You are in the presence of a master in the art of advocacy. From that moment you ought to sit at his feet and observe him carefully. There is no school of advocacy that can furnish superior instruction.

As you might expect, during the recent past my ears have been alert to discover anywhere in the United States some interesting departure from what we would regard here as normal, some little parochialism or provincialism that might add spice to an address of this kind.

I thought I was on the trail of one such practice when, in a Western Federal Circuit, I heard my adversary open his argument by announcing his name, his college, his law school, the law office where he had clerked, and other assorted items of his *curriculum vitae*. I myself belong to a school that doesn't even practice the Geneva Convention. I don't even give my name, rank, or serial number. Here, I thought, was an amusing parochialism with which to entertain my colleagues at the bar association. But this reverie was short-lived. The presiding justice interrupted the biographical disclosures with the curt remark that the court couldn't care less and asked counsel to please proceed to the argument.

Once I discovered that the style of argument was to a significant degree affected by the character of the appellate tribunal, I attempted to separate those institutional characteristics, as distinguished from personal characteristics, which probably contributed to this differentiation. After some trial and error in the process of selection, I identified four attributes that deserved, in my opinion, special attention:

First, the size of the court's membership.

Second, the stability of that membership.

Third, the court's jurisdiction to review findings of fact.

Fourth, the degree of finality of the decisions of the tribunal.

Perhaps good advocacy would prompt me to keep you in suspense concerning the generalizations that I formulated with respect to each of these factors. I shall not employ that pedagogic device. I will state to you right now the four generalizations that I have distilled out of materials that do not readily lend themselves to classification. After all, the art of persuasion is a personal and idiosyncratic art in which individuality plays a major role. This much, however, I believe I can safely assert as generalizations.

First, the higher the court, the lower the pitch of the argument, the less strident its tone, the smaller the role of the brasses and drums. If I were to put it in mathematical terms, I would say that the pitch of argument varies in inverse proportion to the altitude of the court.

The second generalization is that the greater the degree of finality to the court's decision, the more the argument will stress what the law ought to be. In the mixture of law and prophecy that makes up all appellate argument, there is more precedent and less prophecy at the lower end of the finality spectrum and more prophecy and less precedent at the higher end of that spectrum. If I were to state this in mathematical terms, I would say that the prophetic ingredient of the argument varies in proportion to the degree of finality to the court's decision.

Third, whether the court has jurisdiction to review findings of fact will affect the substance of the argument but not the style. In either case, facts are the most sophisticated tools of the advocate before every reviewing tribunal. This rule I have reduced to a doggerel:

> One maxim above all pray keep intact:
> You may be a great rhetorician,
> A most extraordinary dialectician;
> Your smile quite seductive,
> Your logic all inductive;
> But to make your point incisive,
> Sharpened till it's decisive,
> There is nothing like a fact.
> Clean or grubby,
> Slim or chubby,
> There is nothing like a fact.

My fourth generalization is that the bigger the court's membership and the more stable its composition, the more it develops institutional preferences which it is prudent to observe.

Let us now take some of these characteristics in turn and see what they yield on inspection. First, there is size of membership. As you know, appellate courts in the United States vary in size. We have courts of one, three, five, seven, and nine judges. I don't know of any court of larger dimensions in the United States, although I have seen larger courts outside the United States and there used to be some domestic courts which had some lay members that made them larger.

When the art of persuasion is well practiced, it will inevitably appear that an argument that is addressed to a one-man court will be more precisely tailored to the views, preferences, habits of mind, and even the idiosyncracies of the single judge than an argument addressed to a court of large membership. That seems to me to be self-evident.

However, the full range or the full application of this range of capability is in practice diminished, especially in large cities like New York, Chicago, and Los Angeles. One cause of this is that the lawyer is often unable to forecast the identity of the judge who will hear the argument. Another is that it is not always possible for the lawyer to be familiar with the habits, preferences, and views of one particular judge for the very reason that he is a member of a large panel.

A visiting lawyer, admitted *pro hac vice*, who argues before a single judge is under tremendous handicap. I think he needs very careful coaching and instruction in the personality of this tribune. Under these circumstances it is of the utmost importance that the visiting lawyer acquaint himself with as much of the judge's written output as possible, when the identity of the judge is predictable.

To enter a courtroom without an awareness of the particular judge's performance in the very area of the law under discussion is, in my view, to court disaster. To illustrate, suppose you are before a one-man court that is reviewing a referee's report. Surely a careful advocate will ascertain whether the reviewing judge appointed the referee and whether, if he appointed him, it was because he held that referee in especially high esteem or because he yielded to the demands of political patronage. This information may guide the argument away from the claimed misbehavior of the referee to the asserted injustice of his decision.

The possibility of tailoring an argument to the special taste of the judges diminishes as the membership of the tribunal increases. With courts of very large membership, like the Supreme Court of the United States, undue catering to the known preferences of one judge may very well alienate the others. In courts of large membership the preferred course, in my opinion, is to take heed of the frequently unwritten, sometimes unspoken, preferences of the particular court as an institution rather than as a group of individuals.

My second point was stability of membership. Men who work closely together for any considerable period of time develop a dominant code of preferred advocacy. If the membership of the court is stable, as for instance in the Supreme Court of the United States or in the New York Court of Appeals, it is possible by close observation and reading to divine that which is generally frowned on and that which gains favor.

The greatest difficulty in discovering and responding to these subtle but powerful aids to persuasion is encountered in courts that operate by a system of panels of varying membership. A prime example is the Court of Appeals for the Second Circuit. A secondary example is the Appellate Division of this judicial department. The fact that the identity of the panel is frequently not revealed until very close to the time of argument and, indeed, is sometimes changed on the very day of argument requires not only considerable foreknowledge of the bench as a whole but a capacity for flexibly adjusting oneself to a new set of conditions.

There is no escaping the thrall of the rule that a change

of personnel of a reviewing tribunal is a change of conditions. To plow along with an argument tailored for one group of minds and deliver it unchanged to another group of minds is to misjudge the function of oral argument. To omit the attempt to shape the argument to a particular group of minds is to abdicate the function of advocacy altogether.

I would suppose that it is self-evident that, to be persuasive, an argument designed for the ears of a panel composed, say, of Learned Hand, Augustus Hand, and Jerome Frank would have to be altered considerably in direction, scope, and style if it turned out that the panel consisted of Charles Clarke, Harry Chase, and Thomas Swan. However, if you asked me *how* to redesign the argument so as to meet this change of circumstances I have just suggested, I would be as tongue-tied as if you asked me what it is that the true Parisienne does to her beret to make it look saucy when it looks so insipid on the head of a girl from Dubuque.

All I can safely say is that if the advocate intimately knows the membership of the tribunal, he allows that knowledge to intermingle with and influence his own style. If he is a great advocate, the additional ingredient will homogenize with everything else he brings to the argument. The end product will be, not a sycophantic submission to another's mind, but an artistic expression of the advocate's own personality, sharpened and focused to accomplish its mission of winning the mind of the tribunal to his view of the problem and its solution.

The third item is capacity to review facts. On superficial, a priori reasoning, one would suppose that a great chasm would divide appellate courts that review facts from those that do not. My observation has persuaded me that there is no such gap. Of course, in one case the advocate may urge the court to take a different view of evidence from that which his adversary urges. This, however, refers to the object of the attempt to persuade, not to its manner.

I have heard lawyers, bemused by the rule that a particular court will not review findings of fact, proceed as if that court were not interested in fact. Arguments pitched in the form of a contest between pure and abstract principles, unsullied by any earthy contact with human facts and behavior, are generally disastrous. Conceivably they may form a significant portion of the written brief. In oral argument they are an abomination. For oral argument, there is no substitute for a narrative of events that moves the heart and the mind in favor of the cause advocated.

And finally we come to finality. In my mind the one attribute that above all others differentiates appellate courts is the degree of finality that attaches to their judgments. It measures the quantum of power that the court wields. And power is a form of energy that pervades every molecule of its possessor. Consequently, it enters not only into its every act but into the form and mode in which it conducts its activity.

Since this attribute differentiates the courts, it necessarily should and does differentiate the form, style, and content of the argument. The most easily recognizable deficiency in an argument, one that you notice at once, is that it is off-key. And when is it off-key? When it appears to be addressed to a tribunal having less or more power in terms of finality than the court actually addressed.

This point, so easily generalized, is peculiarly difficult to particularize. Just how do you reshape your argument, which was so successful in the Appellate Division, for the Court of Appeals? What do you say to the United States Supreme Court that you would not say to the Circuit Court of Appeals? It seems to me that a brief inspection of each of these tribunals might be instructive in this area.

Let's turn to the Appellate Division, First Department. I suppose that this court is the busiest appellate tribunal in the world. I have not based this supposition on a study of any statistics. This is a conclusion I have reached on the basis of observation.

The judges who serve that bench are selected from among the Supreme Court justices. That alone would tend to create a bench of above-normal competence and capacity. But regardless of prior experience, a judge of that tribunal is exposed to so vast a volume and variety of judicial raw material that he soon achieves a very high order of expertise. Expertise, of course, is not the equivalent of wisdom.

The Appellate Division is a court where judicial familiarity with the major and minor principles of the law may be taken for granted, where the shorthand language of the practitioners of any speciality may be freely used to accelerate argument. In short, an argument in the Appellate Division, at its best, is a conversation between professionals, in the jargon of the profession, in which the obvious, the familiar, the well-accepted propositions need not be argued or, indeed, even stated.

Because invariably the Appellate Division judges have had trial experience, unlike those in other appellate tribunals, they have an awareness of the lawyer's problems in litigation, with a vastly greater immediacy of appreciation than judges of other appellate courts. For instance, the United States Supreme Court cannot possibly be acquainted with the local practices and professional habits of the fifty states of the Union, as are the judges, for instance, of the Appellate Division of the First Department with respect to the habits and practices of this department. In this sense too, therefore, I speak of the Appellate Division as a body of pros, knowledgeable, sophisticated, and subtly sensitive to the procedural niceties, to the virtuosity of the particular lawyer's approach to a problem. Moreover, they are less dependent than, say, the Justices of the Supreme Court of the United States on the instruction furnished them by counsel concerning local practice.

If you think there are no differences in local practice, let me report that recently I tried to discontinue an action by consent in the state of Texas. I had two formal opinions from two law firms in the state of Texas advising me how to do it. I think getting a prisoner out of Dannemora on a writ of coram nobis is simple compared with obtaining a discontinuance by consent in Texas.

In the Appellate Division, First Department, an argument is a two-way conversation. But no matter how brisk the exchange, you cannot escape the judicial awareness that it is a court of *intermediate* appeal, that what it says will be inspected by higher authority, that it must not only be a shaper of policy but a forecaster of the policy that our higher court will shape.

How much restraint this puts on the imagination of any particular judge is beyond the capacity of a mere lawyer to gauge. That the tribunal as an institution is under a sense of restraint is amply supported, I believe, by the history of the court.

As a professional experience, I would say that today an argument in the First Department is of unique quality. It was not always so. I can remember when it was quite different.

Today you find yourself addressing a panel of five judges who know your record, who have reflected on the competing difficulties presented by each of the contending solutions. Anyone who thinks that he can stand at the bar of that court and read an argument prepared for him by a junior has a startlingly disquieting surprise in store for him. I do not mean that he will necessarily lose his case. After all, the merits may be so clearly on his side that he cannot lose. But he will know that the judges know that he has not done his homework; and somehow, in some subtle way, that intelligence will be communicated to everybody in that courtroom.

One slight flaw, if I may respectfully say so, detracts from the pleasure of the adventure in the First Department. One senses a pressure of time. Sometimes you acquire an extrasensory perception that if you did not quite consume all the time allotted to you, you would win judicial favor. I realize, of course, that it is difficult to stuff the meat of five hours of argument into a four-hour sausage. What amazes me is how successfully the First Department performs this piece of magic, day after day. In my judgment, there is no better place for a young advocate to win his spurs than in the Appellate Division, First Department.

And now a word about the New York Court of Appeals. Personally, I have always found the courtroom of the New York Court of Appeals the most delightful place in which to make an argument. The room is serene. The illumination is adequate. Space for counsel is generous. The judges are uncommonly courteous. For reasons I have never been able to explain, I undergo an aesthetic experience every time I attend there. Perhaps the awareness that I am in one of the greatest common-law courts in the world, where one can see the historic, liberating system of law in the very act of its creativity, is that which fills me with awe and excitement.

The New York Court of Appeals does have the final word on the law that governs a state of imperial proportions, except for a minute segment that is reviewable by the Supreme Court of the United States. To such a court it is of course always permissible to speak of the law that ought to be. The precedents are there, and the power to overrule is available in adequate magnitude. To such a court it is always permissible to speak of the symmetry of the grand design as the law is shaped, case by case, decision by decision, of the trend and direction of development, of new needs and wants that require enfoldment under the capacious tent of the common law.

It is folly to approach that court without very precise study of the scope of its jurisdiction and reviewing power in your case. In answer to the question from the chief judge, "How did you get here?" it is not correct to answer that you drove up on the Thomas E. Dewey Thruway. It is both folly and discourtesy to deliver a jury speech to that court. It will surely win no votes. You are fortunate if the judges will attribute such misconduct to your ignorance rather than to the vulnerability of your case.

As far as I know, the New York Court of Appeals has never announced whether as a regular practice the judges read the briefs in advance of argument. Corridor gossip suggests that, for any particular case, one or more of the judges may have read the briefs. This opinion is supported by the form of questioning in that court, which may vary from a simple question of fact to sophisticated inquiries that touch the very heart of the problem.

There is no question that organizing an argument for a court of which some members are fully conversant with the case while others are thumbing the briefs to discover whether it relates to habeas corpus or to goods sold and delivered is an exceedingly difficult assignment. My suggestion is that it is a difficulty that should be taken into account. It is not solved by lack of awareness of it.

The Court of Appeals, of course, is both professionally and historically one of tremendous eminence. Its decisions command respect in a great community of courts. In addressing such a court, it seems to me that flippancy of speech or levity, except of the most adroit quality, is out of place. I have heard it tried. The impression created was, to say the least, painful. A seasoned lawyer will treat an opportunity to argue in that court as one that commands his best deportment, his finest choice of expression, and a chance to exhibit a gallant and chivalrous mode of argumentation.

A very singular tribunal is the Court of Appeals for the Second Circuit. Nine active judges now serve that court, one or more senior judges sit from time to time, and occasionally district judges are impressed into service. The judges sit in changing panels of three and in an order designed to produce the greatest possible pattern of variety. I have not done the calculation to determine how many possible combinations are available, but it is likely that every argument you make will to some extent be before a different court.

Unless one argues there with an unusual degree of frequency, it is impossible to catch the spirit of each and every possible panel. And these panels are different; at least so they seem to the advocate. The panel of that court at which Harold Medina presides is quite a different institution from the one at which Judge Kaufman presides.

By reason of this constant change in the pattern of membership, it is not possible for the bar to discover a solid institutional formula that is calculated to cater to the known preferences of the majority. Manifestly, if I were preparing, say, an argument for Judge Moore alone, it would be different from an argument designed for Judge Friendly alone.

The task is complicated and made vastly more difficult by the circumstance that the Court of Appeals for the Second Circuit does not announce the membership of the panel until the Friday preceding the date of argument. If your argument is scheduled for Monday or Tuesday, I would suppose that by the preceding Friday you have pretty well made up your mind about what you are going to say.

The Second Circuit Court of Appeals is of course different from the New York Court of Appeals in that, to a vastly greater degree, its decisions are reviewable by the

United States Supreme Court. That is one major difference. Another is that it operates in a national context in which it is one of eleven courts of equal rank. Such a court cannot quite achieve the status of lawgiver that the New York Court of Appeals can assert. To such a court a more constant question is what the law *is*.

When you are in new territory and the question is what the law ought to be, it is not enough to show, in the Second Circuit, that what you propose would be responsive to the needs of an intensely urbanized, industrialized seaboard society of heterogeneous origin. It must also meet the test of validity in societies different in makeup, orientation, and activity. If the proposed rule is suggested as appropriate to Vermont, the question is: How will it serve New York, California, Idaho, and Louisiana? If a new public policy is being fabricated on the anvils of advocacy, it may not suffice that it gives legal sanction to the ethics and mores of Brooklyn, where the appeal may have originated. Does it lag behind or leap too far ahead of what should be the public policy of New Haven?

The Court of Appeals for the Second Circuit has on occasion informally announced from the bench that the judges are familiar with the record and the briefs. For reasons I do not quite comprehend, that fact has not been absorbed by the bar in quite the way in which it has learned of the practice of the Appellate Division, First Department. It is my observation that many advocates appearing in that court do not seem to be aware of the practice of the judges of that court to read briefs in advance.

Whenever there is misunderstanding between bar and bench concerning that fact, there is bound to be generated a degree of tension in which the court feels it is being subjected to unnecessary oratory while, of course, the advocate thinks he is telling the judges what they must have for the decision.

Historically and currently, the Second Circuit Court of Appeals has been staffed by many men of very superior talent. It is only natural that it should demand the most of those who appear before it. Sometimes its disappointment is made quite manifest, but so also is its pleasure when it hears a truly persuasive argument. My private advice is that it is no place for amateurs.

Now a word about the Supreme Court of the United States. The outstanding characteristic of the Supreme Court is its supremacy. Its decisions are not subject to review in any other court. The substantial portion of its work involving constitutional questions is not subject to any revision at all except by constitutional amendment.[1] Its statutory and constitutional exegesis is the supreme law of the land.

Mr. Justice Jackson once quipped: "The Court is not supreme because infallible, but infallible because supreme." Both the disposition of cases on the merits and the invocation of the Court's discretionary jurisdiction are inevitably affected by the burden of such infallible supremacy.

The cases before the Court are generally difficult. They involve the resolution of close questions and the adjustment of important interests. The Court is keenly aware that it is molding the law, that by and large its word is the last

[1] Of 114 full opinions of the Court disposing of cases on the merits in the 1964 term, a constitutional question comprised the principal issue in 53. *The Supreme Court, 1964 Term*, 79 Harv L Rev 56 at Table II (1965).

word, and that it needs all the help it can get from counsel.

The atmosphere at oral argument is that of a seminar, not a lecture. The Justices frequently discuss the issues with counsel in a most active and lively fashion. Counsel should be prepared to enter into the spirit of the inquiry. Not only in argument but also in seeking review and in briefing the merits of a case, counsel best serve their clients by manifesting their willingness to help the Court face and solve the difficult problems with which it is confronted.

That Court is unquestionably more concerned with developing general propositions of law than in resolving particular disputes of mine and thine. As you know, the Court can hear only a small fraction of the cases that are urged upon it and may be able to touch a particular area of the law only at rare intervals.

Because of the Court's need to take a broad and long-run view, Justices frequently ask hypothetical questions going well beyond the facts of the case before them. Very seldom is it wise to say to the Court, in answer to a question, "The Court need not reach that question in this case." More than once a Justice has replied, "I do need to reach it."

Cases before the Supreme Court commonly present a conflict between two competing interests both of which represent important values to the community. Indeed, it is the difficulty inherent in resolving that conflict that normally warrants the grant of certiorari or, on appeal, demonstrates the substantiality of the federal question. It is a mistake to fail to see the legitimacy of the value represented by your adversary or hope that it will not be

seen by the Court. It is much wiser and better practice to
recognize the difficulty of resolving the conflict and to
show why it should be settled in your favor.

Virtually every case that comes to the Supreme Court
has lurking in it a key question that represents a real
difficulty or embarrassment for counsel. You may be sure
that question will be asked. A remarkable number of lawyers seem to hope that they will not be confronted with
the obvious difficulty. They will be confronted. To be
caught off-balance by such a question not only involves
missing a precious opportunity to guide the Court's thinking but also leaves the impression that you have not taken
seriously the problem with which the Court is wrestling.
A well-prepared and well-reasoned answer that candidly
acknowledges the troublesome aspects of the question but
leads the Court toward the desired solution does all that
oral advocacy can do.

I think it was Dean Acheson who quoted a Solicitor
General who, when asked that kind of question, said "Ah,
your Honor, how often I have asked myself that question;
and more and more seek its answer along this way." From
then on, a common search for truth and light were entered upon by Court and counsel.

That Court, the Supreme Court, is the Supreme Court
of the United States. Its writ runs through a vast, heterogeneous continent. The matters appearing before it come
from all points between Anchorage and Key West. The
Court appears to be conscious of its lack of familiarity with
all the variant customs, procedures, mores, and institutions which flourish across the nation and which may have
material bearing on the cases it must decide. Furthermore,

the Court cannot hope to achieve more than a limited familiarity with the record in every case. For these reasons the Court is highly dependent on information and illumination supplied by counsel.

The direct result is that nothing can destroy a lawyer's effectiveness faster than a hint of a lack of complete candor. Upon receiving a statement of fact that seemed less than frank, Justices have been seen to throw up their hands in a gesture of dismissal, leaving all present to understand that the overzealous advocate was discredited and might as well sit down for all the good he could do his client by further argument.

Counsel must know with precision what is in the record and that it is the record. They must be able to supply reasonably uncontroversial information even if it is not in the record and always with indubitable accuracy.

Some Justices appear to read the briefs and even the record before argument. Others do not. The only thing you can do in the Supreme Court is to assume that the Justices do not know what the case is about. It is best to tell them promptly and concisely at the outset how the issue relates to a general problem in which they are interested.

In view of the fact that the Justices meet on Friday to vote on cases that were heard Monday through Thursday, you can see that your argument plays a tremendous role in shaping their minds. Insofar as they can be persuaded, you had better persuade them right then and there.

The Court's time is very precious, and the time that it allots to you should be precious to you. It is a crime to waste it. Time taken in the Supreme Court to tell a joke or an anecdote, no matter how apt, would only evoke frigid irritation. A prefatory complaint about how your adversary did not serve the brief on time is, of course, a total waste of time and may even be worse: the Justices may actually get exercised about it and take away the rest of the time you have for argument.

On the plane homeward bound after an argument in the Supreme Court, you will of course be thinking about your presentation and you will then formulate a vastly more sparkling response to the Justice's inquiry than the one you actually rendered. Two years later, when you narrate the story of your victory, unconsciously that sparkling response will be part of the narrative. That is as it should be. After all, sparkling responses should be preserved like decorative swords, even if never used in actual battle.

Few lawyers, except possibly the Solicitors General, can count a very large number of arguments in the Supreme Court. It would seem to me wise to treasure each such occasion and so to use it that you can look back on it with pride in your performance, regardless of whether it led to victory or to defeat.

There are, of course, many additional respects in which appellate courts can be compared. I remember an occasion in one of the Southern Circuits when after the argument the entire bench descended into the well of the court and visited with the lawyers. Whether this is its regular practice or was an act of special hospitality to the lawyers from remote jurisdictions, I do not know, but what a heart-warming experience it was!

I have been in another appellate court where the climate was so frigid that a fur coat would have been the appropriate garb. Again, I do not know whether that is the court's normal temperature or whether it was an expression of distaste for the invasion of its precincts by foreign lawyers.

As between courts that sit in sphinxlike silence and courts that unduly interrupt, my own preference is for the latter. Indeed, I believe that most appellate advocates favor questions from the bench. Naturally they prefer questions that advance the argument rather than those that simply reveal want of attention on the part of the judge.

I cannot find fault with those lawyers who object to appellate judges who, during argument, read the record or the brief or answer personal correspondence. But as far as falling asleep is concerned, that is a fault that I attribute entirely to counsel. If the judge falls asleep, it is because counsel has not kept him awake.

Some courts exude an aura of distinction and prestige that tends to extract from those who appear before them their maximum performance. The Supreme Court of the United States, of course, belongs to that category by virtue of its occupancy of the apex of the judicial hierarchy. Every now and then, however, some court of lesser eminence achieves that capacity to elicit the best from the bar. That was certainly true of the court of which Learned Hand was the chief. I do not know of a single lawyer who did not feel called on to screw his preparation one turn tighter, whose intellectual antennae were not vibratingly alert, when he knew he was to address a court over which Learned Hand presided. The same was true of the New York Court of Appeals when Chief Judge Cardozo was its presiding officer. I speak only of the past. It would be presumptuous for me to speak of those presently occupying similar roles. It is one of the glories of our profession that from its ranks have risen many judges who belong to such a hall of fame.

Comparing all the courts I have addressed, I would say, my friends, that none of them is staffed by angels, and for that I am duly grateful. I would say that the distribution of genius is about normal for the professional community of which the judiciary is a part. In my judgment, however, the distribution of intelligence is substantially above normal for the judiciary. All you have to do is compare a group of judges with a group of professors, executives, or any other topflight body of professional men. They are not in the same league. The judges outshine them every time, and I do not mean to pour ointment on anybody's head.

Almost universally the judges work long and hard with material much of which is tedious and all of which is difficult. All the judges I have ever encountered appreciate help in the form of a good brief and an effective argument.

I would say that we in the United States enjoy access to a relatively high quality of judicial performance. If you have any doubt about it, do what I once did. I stood on the place where the Sermon on the Mount was delivered, and I asked myself how far I would have to travel beyond the borders of the small land I was in before I would find a court to whose care I would be willing to entrust my liberty or my fortune. Thank you.

QUESTION PERIOD

QUESTION: I wonder if I might ask Judge Rifkind three short questions:

1. Have you ever had occasion to have a record of your argument prepared and submitted for any reason to the court after argument?

2. What is your view, if any, on the use of physical evidence for an appellate argument?

3. Lastly, do you find from court to court that there are any vast differences on motions for reargument?

JUDGE RIFKIND: Well, as to the transcript of an argument, I have never submitted to an appellate court a transcript of my oral argument. We generally submit a printed brief, of course. My object in making an argument is just one—to have the court go into the chambers and say, "I think that fellow is right; let me start working on that hypothesis." If I have achieved that, I have achieved the function of my oral argument. Of course, you can start a resolution of the question on either hypothesis.

Physical evidence, if by that you mean charts, graphs, and things of that kind, I have used both in trial courts and in appellate courts, but more rarely, of course, in appellate courts than in trial courts. But I don't know about other kinds of physical evidence. I don't normally engage in the personal-injury business in which that sort of thing is used most frequently.

Your last question has to do with motions for reargument. Of course it has become a practice in the Federal Court of Appeals, because of the new rule, to make motions for reargument in almost every case. One of these days I suppose that court will have to rid itself of that practice because it will become a nuisance, I assume. It also becomes a nuisance for the bar because you feel obliged to make a motion for reargument in every case you lose. But I am not aware that there is any special practice. As you know, very rarely is a motion for reargument successful, and I think that is the universal experience.

QUESTION: Judge Rifkind, can you tell us how and to what extent a dissent in an intermediate appellate court would influence or affect your argument either in the Court of Appeals or in the United States Supreme Court?

JUDGE RIFKIND: Of course, if you are the appellant, there is a great comfort in having the assistance of a good dissent, and anybody who doesn't take advantage of it is missing an opportunity.

There are rare occasions, you know, when you have to detach yourself from even a victorious decision and try to sustain it on other grounds. I am not being facetious about that. I just had that experience within the last few days; so I know whereof I speak.

I think the idea that you must necessarily accept the winning decision of the court below as the unfailing guide to what moves the appellate court is a mistake. Use it for what it can do for you. The same is true of a dissenting opinion. However, there is no question but that once you have a dissent and if you are the appellant, you have got a point of leverage which is of tremendous significance.

QUESTION: Judge Rifkind, I think in some jurisdictions the appellate court must write an opinion in every case. Don't you believe it would be a good rule in our department, except in a very, very simple matter, for that to be the practice also?

JUDGE RIFKIND: I can't imagine a more deplorable rule than one that would command the production of more opinions than are now being produced. The opinions that really reveal a new truth, point a new direction, create a new departure, are mighty few. So many of them could well have said "Affirmed" and a string of authority. Many opinions I suspect are written to satisfy the demands of counsel's advocacy; that is all. No, I would rather see fewer opinions written than more.

QUESTION: Sir, on appeal what use, if any, do you make of the fact that a judge whose decision you may be appealing is to your knowledge perhaps not the best of lower court judges?

JUDGE RIFKIND: What use do I make of it? I assume you don't keep the identity of the trial judge a secret from the appellate body, and if you have that opinion of him and if it is shared by the bar, I think the appellate court probably knows about it. But that is not necessarily an item in your favor, you know. You can only go two ways, and he might be right.

References Made by Judge Rifkind

Acheson, Dean, *Morning and Noon*, Boston, Houghton Mifflin, 1965, p. 99.

Shakespeare, William, *Much Ado about Nothing*, Act III, scene 5.

A Summing Up

**CHARLES D. BREITEL, Chairman,
and the Lecturers**

Charles D. Breitel, a judge of the New York
Court of Appeals, is a graduate of the Columbia
Law School. He was an assistant district attorney
on the staff of Thomas E. Dewey and later
served as counsel to Governor Dewey. He
has served as a justice of the Supreme Court of
the State of New York and of the Appellate Division
of the Supreme Court (1950–1967). He is a
member of The Association of the Bar of the City
of New York and of the New York County, New
York State, and American Bar Associations. He is
a member of the Council of the American Law
Institute and has served on the Advisory Committee
on the Model Penal Code. He is also a member of
the President's Commission on Crime.

PANEL

CHARLES D. BREITEL, *Chairman*
SIMON H. RIFKIND
SAMUEL E. GATES
WHITMAN KNAPP
HARRIS B. STEINBERG
MILTON POLLACK

JUDGE BREITEL: This, as you know, of course, is the last of the series on appellate advocacy, in which six distinguished advocates have tried to tell us what they know about appellate advocacy. It has been a remarkable series. The purpose was not primarily to tell you how to do it but to try to study in depth what this process of appellate advocacy is.

One of the things we had in mind at the very beginning was that we wanted lawyers who practiced as appellate advocates to try to tell us about the process. In the literature and in the lectures that have been given in this area over many, many decades, there has been a tendency to ask judges rather than lawyers to speak. This was a wrong approach; after all, what judges thought they wanted from advocates was not necessarily what advocates should do or did do.

I should now express a caveat. What advocates think they do or should do is likewise not necessarily what they really do or what they ought to do. The whole effort in this series has been to have an analysis of much greater depth than the analyses made in the past, and even if we found that lawyers didn't know nearly as much as they thought they knew, at least we should get some new dimension of this problem. Even if we did not discover any pat eternal truths of jurisprudential value or any techniques of great practical value, unquestionably we should learn something about the process. I think we have been successful.

One of the assumptions made in arranging the series was that neither all classes of appeals nor all appellate courts were alike. We felt that the assumption of many discussions in the past that there was a common technique to be used in a common experience was undoubtedly false.

Our assumption has been validated beyond anyone's expectations. It's been proved beautifully by our lecturers in discussing the different kinds of appeals and the different kinds of courts in which lawyers appeal.

Now, what I should like to do tonight is to highlight some of the common elements in the six lectures. I know that I shall not do justice to them, and this is not merely a lawyer's reservation. I have tested my talk on myself seven times, and I just can't do it in the relatively limited time that is available.

I shall also try to highlight what I regard as some of the paradoxical aspects of the six lectures. Then I thought it might be useful if I just cracked the door a little bit so that you might see what at least one judge and maybe some other judges would like to see happen in an appellate argument. Lastly, I would hope that from my attempts we might create a conversation among the members of this panel.

Now, what are some of the common elements in the lectures?

The first I have referred to already when I said that we worked on the assumption that cases fell in different kinds of classes and that courts fell in different kinds of classes, but the lecturers went well beyond this point. They proved that not only courts and judges and classes of appeals but also individual cases and individual lawyers require and use entirely separate and distinct techniques.

It was impossible to say that you should do this in this kind of case before this kind of court because this was what I would do. Every single one of the lecturers, without exception, talked of the techniques of appellate advocacy as requiring a very special kind of application to the particular case in the class of case in which it lay and to the particular court with the particular judges constituting that court, as well as to its jurisdiction.

The second common element that appeared in each of the lectures, with a unanimity that was remarkable, was the essentiality of oral argument. Sometimes this was even emphasized as a result of questions that came from the floor; just about every man said, "I can't understand a person offering to submit in a case; I would always want to argue."

Yet you could tell from the questions that came from the floor that there are innumerable lawyers who ask, "What is the value of oral argument?" But here is this counsel from each one of our lecturers, all of whom are good oral arguers, that oral argument is essential.

I would step away from my classification for a moment and suggest to you that this seeming paradox results from the fact that some people are not capable of oral argument. Then I would suggest something else that I hope to advert to again: that some cases may not be capable of being argued; and that if either one of these two things happens and especially if the two happen in conjunction, of course you cannot argue. But then the real question is: What are you doing in court?

Now all the lawyers agreed with an absolute unanimity that the function of oral argument—and I would suggest also of the printed argument, although in that sense I use what I am going to say somewhat figuratively—is to engage the court. By engaging the court, I don't mean keeping the judges awake. I do mean that you get the judges into a discussion with the lawyers about the case and the issues in the case. An argument that does not do that is a failure.

I think it is not unfair to say that there was agreement about this, even with regard to what was described by Mr. Gates as the "cold bench," the bench that does not read the briefs in advance, just as it is terribly true of the "hot bench," the bench that does read the briefs in advance.

The thing that was most interesting to me was the fact that all of the six lecturers stressed the search for motivation. I don't mean crass, corrupt, subterranean, or libidinal motivations on the part of the court but motivations based on a legal philosophy, an economic philosophy, a political philosophy, or a notion of statesmanship on the part of the court.

I suppose that in the middle of this century searching for motivation sounds like a commonplace, but truly it is not. It means that we have in practice a conscious adherence to a realistic philosophy, a notion that courts do not decide cases by simply applying some rules of law found in black letter in books, nor do they apply these rules of law simply to sets of facts arranged in convenient legalized categories. It means that there is movement in the court toward some sort of goal and that unless the advocate detects that movement and tries to get the court to move in the direction in which he thinks it ought to move on behalf of his client, the advocacy will be ineffective.

This is an important comment, and I would suggest to you that it has a tremendous import from the point of view of legal philosophy. It has an even greater import from the point of view of the techniques of the advocate in the argument of a case orally and in print.

So it doesn't surprise us that if you have fifty cases in your favor, that is not the end of the matter. All our lectures stressed this. Judge Rifkind analyzed the problem against a background of the different kinds of courts that have different amounts of leeway, different freedoms, in satisfying these different motivations.

The one in this lecture series who didn't stress motivation so much, oddly, was Thurgood Marshall. The reason I say "oddly" is that, among the six men, the man who did more than any of them to change the direction of the courts in this country was Thurgood Marshall and yet this was not one of the things that he selected as something of tremendous importance in advocacy.

All our lecturers stressed the importance of not separating law from facts. One or two told stories of their youth or of observations of other young men who had tried to categorize the argument of a case into law and into facts and the awful fates that befell them. The lecturers thought of the law and the facts as being united as a man is to his skin; they couldn't separate them but had to discuss them together as part of an organic whole.

All, interestingly, stressed the resistance to reversal by appellate courts and the fact that the appellants' burden was much heavier. They even, in a sense, wept tears for appellants and apparently took no joy in the happiness of respondency.

In varying degrees they stressed the importance and function of oral argument to a hot bench and a cold bench and the effect it would have on the significance of the brief, which, almost all agreed, was the permanent, persisting argument of the advocate before the court, in the language of Thurgood Marshall.

In varying degrees the speakers—but most markedly Judge Rifkind, in a way that I think was a unique contribution—stressed the effect of the level of the court and its structure. This makes a tremendous difference. Judge Rifkind also commented on the effect that results from the difference in the number of judges who sit on a bench and what he referred to as the stability of the court, that is, whether the members change from time to time.

Some of the speakers stressed the importance, in the developing of one's advocacy techniques, of whether the court has power to review facts; and I would add, to review things besides facts, because all the powers of review are not divided simply into just law and facts. This makes a difference in how a case is argued, both orally and in print.

Lastly and most importantly, there is the matter of the finality with which the court speaks. It is one thing to argue a point of novel law in a court that has a very restricted power to make novel law. It is quite another story to argue that case in a court that has the power not only to make novel law but to undo existing law. The range of that advocacy is entirely different, and you just do not argue the case in the same way in both courts. Yet I have seen lawyers do exactly that. I have had them come into my court, an intermediate court, and argue that a decision handed down by the state Court of Appeals only a matter of several months ago was wrong and that we should disregard it. This was as nonsensical as asking us if we would promptly walk on the ceiling of the courtroom.

Then of course, from all our lecturers, we had something that, I think, you have always heard from anybody who has ever spoken about appellate advocacy or written on the subject: the need for planning and preparation and the need to anticipate questions from the bench.

Now, those were the common elements that I found in the lectures. I also found some things that were surprising to me as a judge.

The first is that four of the six lecturers talked only about appellants. You would think that there were no respondents in appellate cases and you would think that all respondents were undeserving, that all judges were nasty people who were handing out undeserved rewards to respondents, and that the poor appellants were being regularly abused.

It reminds me that if you talk to a layman about a trial, he is most likely to think of a criminal trial. That, to him, is what a trial is. So here we have sophisticated litigators whom we ask to talk about appellate advocacy, and 80 percent of them think of appellants.

The other interesting thing was that none of the lecturers, with slight exception, talked about how to handle an adversary in his brief. Do you know why? Almost all of them had as their adversary the court. This was the bad fellow. This was the devil. This was the guy who had to be trapped. Not the adversary (he was just a poor fellow earning his fee, but those judges, oh, they were terrible—they were really awful. Maybe the lecturers are right.

All of them, incidentally, without exception, even Thurgood Marshall, assumed that the argument in the brief, as far as the time it took was concerned, was something to be slipped in on a reluctant court. One speaker referred to precious time that should not be wasted. Others talked about the pressure of the court, its business, and the way you had to squeeze these valuable words in and get these printed briefs in so these fellows would read it.

You were like a fellow riding on a carrousel, trying to

throw the ring on the hook: your timing had to be perfect or you lost your opportunity. The lecturers all assumed, without question, that the judges wanted to be left alone. The court didn't want to be disturbed by briefs or by arguments.

Now, this is interesting. I now revert to my more normal role and try to speak about what I think a court wants. I must give you a caveat. I am one judge in one court. We are not alike, even in my court, and my court is not like other courts, structurally, organically, as a matter of constituency.

Nevertheless, I don't think I speak purely from an idiosyncrasy in this respect. The first thing that a court wants is help. The judges have the difficult burden of deciding cases, and the busier the court is, the more help they want. If they are not very busy, they don't need so much help; they have more time. The smarter they are, the more they know they need help. The duller they are, the more they really need help.

Now, in the search for help, I think you will find that just about every judge whom you come across, regardless of the level of the court, has—and I must borrow a timeworn phrase—a categorical imperative to do justice, whatever that may mean. There is not a man, regardless of his background, education, circumstances, or even the reasons or mechanics by which he got to the bench, who doesn't in time rise to the imperative of doing justice in cases, and for this he needs help.

Doing justice is most difficult. As lawyers, we all know this. We simply discover it anew as judges. Now, the kind of help that a judge needs in deciding cases is very simply expressed: He wants a just result in this case by a just procedure. We usually say "a fair procedure." If the procedure is not fair, the thing doesn't work. If the result is not just, it still doesn't work. It's got to be a just result in this case by a fair procedure.

The last rub is the worst of all. It must be a just result that the judge can fairly use in similar cases when they arise in the future. If there weren't all these requirements, especially that last one, it would be an easy job and judges wouldn't need so much help.

Now, this is where lawyers come in with their advocacy. They have got to show the judge that it is a just result, but that is not the whole story. For example, the statute of limitations is against you. How do we get around the statute of limitations? You want to do it in a way that is not fair. Well, you finally solve that problem, but what we want to know is: "Can we do it the same way when the next case comes around?" Answer: "No." You lose.

Now, we want all the help we can get. We want you to talk as long as you can, so long as you are helping us. We want you to write your briefs as long as you can, so long as you are helping us. Later I am going to say more about that qualification, "so long as you are helping us."

The hot bench, by the way, wants the argument in order to bring the lawyers into actual conference with the judges so that they can see whether you can help them. They know what is bothering them. They know the level of their own ignorance, the scope of their own difficulties, or the conceit of their own superiorities but would like to test them on you. The cold bench wants information about the case and also, I think, tries to do exactly what the hot bench tries to do but with less time remaining for the task.

From every advocate, the court, because it needs help in the way I have suggested, wants candor and soundness. That is about the whole story. The judges want you to be honest,

and they want you to be thorough. If you are both, you will
help them. If you aren't, there is no sale.

The members of the court abhor condescension, sometimes expressed by telling them lots of things they already know, or by repetition, which is a waste of time, or by
undue length of argument or brief. What is "undue length?"
That means length that no longer helps in proportion to the
distance involved, in time or in space. If the judges are
busy and if they are tense, undue length becomes objec-
tionable.

If you are helpful, take all the time you want. There is not
a good lawyer who has been doing a good job in arguing a
case who hasn't had this happen to him; when his time for
argument has been exceeded, the judges keep him on his
feet arguing some more. Of course, we have asked for extra
briefs on occasion.

I remember once in my court having a very important
case in which the briefs, from several parties, were literally
about 12 to 18 inches thick. I remember looking forward
to reading them. I took them home, planning to read them
over the Christmas recess. I knew what the problems were
and knew them to be difficult. I expected to be edified by
these books-called-briefs as they explained the issues and the
law to me. I knew that even with the inadequate library I
had at home, there would be no trouble, because everything
would be in the briefs—the length proved that. And then,
the horrors I experienced as I started! I hadn't gone more
than twenty pages in the first brief before I found that it
was useless. I turned to another brief and went another
fifteen or twenty pages and found that was useless, and so
on, through the whole batch. I took them all then and
brought them back to the courthouse. I had wanted to read
them. I had wanted to learn from them, and I didn't object

to their length until I found that they were not helpful. Help is what the court wants.

Now, what about our advocates who want to take on the judges as adversaries? I have only a few comments in that connection. (I am trying to watch my time to be a model to appellate advocates.) What's wrong with having a lot of affirmances? What kind of legal system would we have if most judgments ought to be reversed? I don't think I have to develop that theme at great length. I don't mean that we shouldn't have the appropriate amount of reversals, but I certainly think it proves absolutely nothing to establish that only 17 percent of the cases were reversed or only 21 percent of the cases were reversed, to have our most experienced and distinguished criminal practitioner argue that the situation is worse in the criminal cases than in the civil, and then to have our distinguished civil practitioner say that it's tough even in the civil cases to get a reversal. I don't understand that.

All of us talked about our strategies in handling judges. We must be careful about strategies. I would say in a statement that some of you I fear will take as too simple—but I do not think it is at all simple—that a strategy that is not justified by the merits of the case is just a fancily labeled fallacy. It's just a stunt, and if it is discovered, it spells doom.

So, try to trick the judges if you can, but you'll have to be much smarter than they are. Judge Rifkind said, and I hope he is right, that man for man, occupation for occupation, the judges are better than the others.

Finally, I should like to say something that the advocates who lectured couldn't tell you but that I can tell you, that perhaps the most valuable thing the lawyer brings into the courtroom when he is an advocate is his reputation. His reputation for candor and soundness is worth three points in his brief and a marvelous opening for his oral argument. If his reputation is bad, I don't care what he says or how he says it—he is climbing a glass mountain in shoes covered with oil.

It has to be a reputation for candor and soundness; so watch out for strategies. You see, reputation is related to that other point. Strategy is good if it's justified by the merits of the case. If it is not, it spells doom.

Now I come, happily I hope, to my conclusions. I think the series has demonstrated that there is a value in understanding the nature of advocacy before we even try to determine all the rules that we should use in it and that perhaps the mistake in the past has been that people have sat down to try to write rules without understanding the game.

In this series, we have tried to find out what it is before we have tried to find out how to do it. I should like to suggest that this is quite an essential a priori, that it relates to nothing less important than the preservation of the whole adversary system, because appellate advocacy is just one form of advocacy in the adversary system.

Every time the lawyer functions anywhere in the judicial system, he participates in the adversary system and he is being an advocate. If we have discovered something about how he works or how he should work, then perhaps we have done something to help preserve that system, provided we think it's a good system and one worth keeping. Whether it is worth keeping or not and whether it is good or not, we can find out only by knowing what it is.

For example, if it consists of tricks and strategies to entrap judges and produce wrongful results, then it is no good. If it is a system by which judges are helped most effectively by lawyers representing the sides of their clients, then it is good. There are many viable legal systems throughout the world that do not depend on the adversary system, so let's not assume, you see, that our system is a revealed truth and a practice that could never possibly be changed.

At any rate, that's what we have tried to do, and that's what we have tried to show. To what extent we have been successful, it is obvious that the audience must decide.

Now I hope that I have intrigued the modest members of my panel to come forward and show their mettle.

MR. GATES: Judge, it seems to me that you, tonight, were guilty of a few inconsistencies, if I may say so. I happened to address this group on the hot bench versus the cold bench, and I was interested when you talked a few moments ago about how the court wants help. You said that counsel should not be worried at all about time—the court would bear with him. Then you followed that statement immediately by saying, as a model, "I shall restrict my time."

Now, may I suggest that even if you appear before a hot bench, you have to be prepared to make a cold argument because you can't always be sure that the bench will be quite as hot as you have anticipated. You necessarily contemplate that you will talk ten or fifteen minutes or, by grace, eighteen minutes. Perhaps what you have to say may take as much as twenty minutes. At that point, the court begins to become very impatient. While understanding the burden of the court and the problems you have with repetition, I suggest to you that from time to time you might be somewhat more temperate in the way you watch the clock.

MR. KNAPP: While we are talking about inconsistencies, let me say that before Judge Breitel spoke, he said he was going to point out the fact that we all talked about appellants and said nothing about respondents. He finally did come to that topic. What fascinated me was that in the first few minutes of his talk, when he was discussing oral argument, everything he said on the subject applied only to appellants.

Now, no doubt we did say that the function of oral argument is to engage the court's attention in the issues of the case. That is the function of the appellant. The function of the respondent is to try to avoid oral argument altogether, if he can, but obviously he can't. Therefore, his function is to disengage the court's interest, to let the court feel that there is nothing interesting in the case to hear.

I discussed that problem in considerable detail, and I discussed the techniques to be used. As an example of the appellee's function, take the case that had the most notoriety of any case I ever had—*The Memoirs of Hecate County*—in the Supreme Court of the United States.

Whitney North Seymour argued that case for fifty minutes. He posed every interesting question in the book in such a way that anything I might say about it would make the question look interesting and me stupid. I therefore got up and said three sentences, which boiled down to "Read the book."

Now, I had to say something. I could not insult the court by submitting. My argument, however, if it had gone to any length, would have convinced the court that there was something interesting in the case and we would have lost it.

So, the function of the respondent is to convince the court basically that the case is without interest, that the lower court obviously did a good job and the case should be affirmed, preferably without opinion.

MR. STEINBERG: I was considerably touched by Judge Breitel's plea for help. As one who has spent his life trying to straighten the court out, it seems to me it is a lack of communication that is the trouble.

I am reminded of the cartoon that appeared in the *New Yorker* of the man who was drowning and was shouting, "Au

secours, sauvez moi! Au secours!" Two men on the board-
walk looking down said, "Either that man is a Frenchman
or he is an awful snob."

It is not really a question of their seeking or of our offering
help. Both are true. It is a question of the kind of help they
think they need, not what is available.

It is a fact that the challenge and the interest in this
business is in the appellants' role because you have something
that has already happened in the court below. To sustain it,
as a respondent, you are pretty much bound by what happened there. Even if you think of a better way to do it, you
are stuck with the way the trial court did it and you are
stuck with answering what the appellant says. So while it
is true that most of us spend our time on appellants' behalf,
it seems to me that is the more creative part.

JUDGE RIFKIND: This kind of carrousel-go-round is very enter-
taining. I really don't know that I have had anything to
contribute. I enjoyed immensely what Judge Breitel said. He
made the comment that most of us talked about the burden
of the appellant. Of course we did.

The simple fact is that the statistics make that so. The
appellant's job is the challenging job because, as was pointed
out, so rarely is an appeal won. Therefore, if we are going to
talk to a group of experts full of virtuosity and all that, of
course we will talk about the tough part of the business. We
are not going to belabor what seems to be the easy part.

It reminds me of an occasion on which I was talking to
a group of patent lawyers all of whom were bemoaning the
fact that the courts were so rarely sustaining patents in those
days. I looked around the room and asked the question: "Did
any patent ever go to the burial ground when the pallbearers
were not members of the Patent Bar Association?" Of course,
the answer was that in every case they were members. But

the challenging thing was to sustain the patent, because that was the tough part of the work, and that is why people looked at the situation that way.

I was very much impressed with Judge Breitel's complaint, if I may call it that, that we seem to talk as if judges wanted to be left alone. Well, I'll confess that once you are in the well of the court and are actually engaging them in conversation, they sometimes exhibit the desire for help that he described. But before you get into that well, you start negotiating for the little piece of time that you are going to get, and then it looks as if the Greek gifts that you bear and tender are not particularly appreciated.

I was reminded of this fact this morning when I got two little notices from two appellate courts. In one case I had asked for sixty minutes, and in the other case I had asked for forty-five, which I thought was cutting the time to the bone, you know. The sixty-minute request came back saying I was allowed thirty, and the forty-five–minute request came back saying I was allowed thirty. So, apparently the courts were able to do without my three-quarters of an hour of persuasive argument and survive without my burden of help.

Sometimes that help comes in a form of rapid-fire questioning. This reminds me of the drowning citizen who calls for help and then throws his arms around his rescuer and strangles him. That reach can be very, very long, and the grasp can be very, very tight. Sometimes the demand for help can be positively devastating.

As for the number of reversals, I share Judge Breitel's view of the matter. After all, I have on my desk a little gadget that we call "the decider." It is a coin, very carefully balanced on a prong, which you spin to have it come up "yes" or "no." Sometimes we decide questions by spinning that coin, and it would seem to be a matter of normal probability that if a judge did nothing but rely on the laws of probability, you ought to come out right half the time. Consequently, if you are going to bring about a reversal, you have to have a judge who exceeds that ratio by a considerable amount. Only then do you get a fair chance for a reversal.

I once heard an English judge speaking at one of the judicial conferences who was surrounded by appellate judges. When that was called to his attention, he said: "Well, after all, they exist by the grace of the nisi prius judges. If the nisi prius judges all got together and conspired to commit no error, what would the appellate judges do? They would be out of business."

I recall that the final thing Judge Breitel mentioned was reputation, which he spoke of as being a great asset. I remember at least one judge who said to me that whenever he heard John W. Davis argue a case, he positively closed his mind to his argument for at least a week. He wanted the magic of Davis's voice to subside before he put his mind to the case.

So, sometimes reputation can be a disadvantage. But it is a disadvantage everyone should try very hard to acquire.

MR. POLLACK: One of the things that we all talked about is the problem of whether appeals should be handled on a procedural-error basis or a substantive-error basis. I remember quite well that when Harris Steinberg started this lecture series, he emphasized the importance of following the rules of the game for criminal appeals. Of course, there is such a high regard for personal liberties and personal rights that in arguing appellate matters involving crimes it becomes very important to determine whether the procedural rules have been followed to the letter.

Not so on the civil appeal. On the civil appeal it hasn't been useful in most cases to point out procedural error. Has the substantive rule been applied with substantial justice? That seems to be the more fruitful question.

The civil appeal is generally devoid of the need to support personal liberties or human rights. The impact of a civil judgment on an individual litigant is of less significance on appeal than the satisfaction of a quest for symmetry in the applicable law, no matter what law.

Judge Breitel said that on appeals his court and perhaps many others look for a just result that can fairly be used in similar cases in the future. That is a form of trying to get finality, symmetry, in the law, so that businessmen and others affected by civil litigation will feel that they can point to the rules of *stare decisis.*

This, of course, doesn't lead us to infer that the answers on civil appeals have or could become automatic and thus be programmed for determination, let us say, by a computer. There is still an area of human judgment and perspective and even emotion on civil-appeal matters, and those values cannot be administered by machines.

Our appellate process and its vast entourage exist simply because we are not satisfied to have trial courts render the final decision on civil controversy. Whatever the philosophical reason and whether or not that philosophy prevailed in former ages, the answer today nonetheless is that the initial determination is not regarded, and is not desired to be regarded, even in federal courts, where they have the stringent rule of finality, as a final decision on civil controversies. Yet it is only the exceptional appeal, as has been emphasized time and again here, that succeeds in overturning the initial determination.

In this series, we examined the role and techniques of the advocate. We talked of how he will capture interest and arouse a sense of advocacy in the judge for his cause, because a judge does become an advocate when he gets into the conference room.

We have found that the significant factor here is that the method of the advocate is largely individual, incorporating style, philosophy of persuasion, and even personal sensitivity. It is certainly not a mathematical exercise.

We talked of the courts and those who judge the civil appeal. We raised the question of the tools that are needed for judging modern-day business and social complexities. In this regard, should judges on civil appeals be free to call in disinterested opinions of scholars and scientists and business experts? We raised that question.

On the techniques of judging civil appeals, we have suggested that apprising the parties of the judicial ranking and reformulation of the issues is a problem. Should we be apprised of these before the decisional process has been completed? The purpose of a communication from the bench along these lines would be to afford an effective hearing on the question deemed to be decisive before the judgment on appeal is rendered.

Again, in summing up for the civil appeal, I should emphasize that it must not lapse into a prosaic exercise. The technique must include industry, interest in the task, enthusiasm, belief in the cause, courage to move selectively, creation of a proper plan, organization of solid support and documentation for it, preparation for the kind of tribunal to be faced, a presentation that is simple, brief, and alert with sensitivity, an effort to involve the judge, to make him your advocate for your view, and then prayer.

JUDGE BREITEL: I should like to make a couple of rejoinders here. In the first place, you will notice again, despite all the caveats, that there is a tendency to take on the judge. In other words, there is something peculiar about the relation of bar and bench. There really is.

The interesting thing in our lecture series is that two of our advocates are former judges, Judge Rifkind and Judge Marshall. After a while some special kind of distance develops, and so there is a tendency to take the judge on as the adversary. Whether this is valid or not, good or bad, or just a superficial characteristic of a deeper process, I don't know and I don't care, except that intellectually I think it merits observation and notation because the relation between bar and bench must influence the way the advocates act.

The second thing I should like to refer to is the time point. The time point is important because everything that was said by Mr. Gates and especially by Judge Rifkind about the time point is true and there is a superficial self-contradiction in the things I have said.

But I think I gave the resolution of the contradiction, and that is that it depends on how valuable the help is. By the force of confining your time, by the force of organizing your material, by the force of realizing that you must try to be helpful, you start to make what you have got to say contain sense.

The panel wants to be asked questions.

QUESTION: When the respondent doesn't argue orally, isn't that in a way telling the court that the matter isn't very interesting at all and that time need not be spent on it?

JUDGE BREITEL: Sir, I think I should answer this: That depends on the case. Sometimes when the respondent doesn't answer, we say he hasn't got a thing to say in response. Incidentally, here I would add a comment to Mr. Knapp's point. There are some respondents' cases that are very hard to defend.

They are very challenging, and if you submit on them, it means that you can't defend them.

Every case is different. Every lawyer is different. The court is different. It depends—all I can say is that it depends, it depends, it depends; and this is the most important thing that you can learn about litigation. In the same way that every client is different, every lawyer is different and every judge is different. Therefore, you cannot say that by submitting on a respondent's brief you have suggested that it is unimportant, because nobody may agree with you and you will find that out on decision day.

QUESTION: I should like to ask the panel to help the chairman with his problem about why advocates seem to be anti-judge in their attitude. I wonder if it is not in part a function of the assumption that the more challenging job is the job of the counsel for the appellant, that there is a kind of statistical presumption operating against him, and perhaps also that his job is persuasion and he is not likely to convince his opponent.

MR. STEINBERG: I should say it is true in the appeal of a criminal case that the real adversary of the appellant is not the respondent but the immobility of the court, the desire of the court to ally itself with the interest of society, if you will, with the *status quo*, with the keeping of the whole complex of the criminal process intact and not having it bounced around unduly.

When you come forth with an appellate argument saying that some man is putatively a criminal and guilty of some heinous act and should be set at liberty, you have a heavy burden, not necessarily because of your opponent but because of the court's conscience and the court's identification with the process of criminal law. I have an example in a federal court where some very fine trial judges share the building and affiliate with the appellate court judges. They know each other. They are socially friendly. They regard each other with respect. They come to know each other as decent, able people. That's another factor of immobility against change. You don't like to lecture and correct your colleagues in public any more than you have to.

Vindication of a principle, of an abstract principle of justice, as opposed to the emotions that are let loose by the specifics of a crime is a difficult thing. Witness the *Escobedo* and *Miranda* controversy that has raged in the papers and the oversimplifications—at least, I suggest they may be oversimplifications—that have been offered to the public in many of the discussions of these cases.

So, I say that the real task of the appellant, particularly in a criminal case, is to get beneath the willingness of the appellate court to keep the *status quo*, to engage the judges' sense of injustice, their horror at an injustice, and to use that feeling creatively in the specific case you have that will always be against their individual wishes. The judges are fathers; they are householders; they are simply citizens; they abhor crime as much as anyone else does; and yet their job is to avoid injustice, and in that job they sometimes have to undo what on the record may be a factually proper finding by the court below but one which went against the rules.

QUESTION: I have experienced commencing the argument of an appeal, preparing to outline my facts in the hope that I can convince the court that my side of the case is the one that should have been decided, and after I have talked for about four minutes, one of the judges has said, "We have read your brief. We know the facts." I want to know how to guide myself in preparing the argument.

JUDGE BREITEL: It depends on your case, to begin with. The

case has got to have something. The nature of the case that the lawyer has circumscribes the technique he can apply to it. There is a limit.

You can have a case that has nothing whatsoever to it, and there is nothing you can do with it. We could take all of the five men present tonight, and while they could make the argument much more exciting than you or I could, they still wouldn't be able to make it much of a case. I am not talking about applying ingenuity to something that might be there. It may be that the five fellows may see nothing and then get an expert who may come in and makes the case live. That is different.

But there are some cases that haven't got it. The client that you represent deserves nothing. He has been treated properly by the fairest of judges; a long opinion has been written explaining exactly what is wrong with your client. Now, you have to be a good lawyer, because, to use Llewellyn's words, a poor lawyer can take a case that can sing and make it burp. So the lawyer has to do something with it. If he can't, he ought to hire counsel.

QUESTION: When he starts to develop the facts and gets the comment from the bench, "We have read the brief, and we know the facts," . . .

JUDGE BREITEL: Don't separate the law from the facts. This is deadly. Of course the judges who read the briefs know the facts. By separating the facts from the law, you divide the case in two and each part simply dissolves by itself. You must make them live together. Again and again as the lawyer of ability gets up, he begins to discuss the facts of the case but as he does it, he will also be introducing the questions of law at the same time. They are not separate. The lawyer doesn't give the court a monologue history of the facts and say, "I shall now discuss the law, points 1, 2, and 3."

JUDGE RIFKIND: May I comment on that? It reminds me a little bit of a playwright who was presenting a play to a group of prospective angels. They asked him to give them a few words about what the play was about.

He said, "Well, in Act I, he falls in love with the girl.

"In Act II, he falls in love with the girl.

"And, in Act III, he falls in love with the girl."

One of the prospective angels said, "After you have seen Act I, why do you want to wait and see Act II and Act III?"

The playwright said, "It's a different girl."

When the judge says, "We have read your brief, and we know the facts," you go on to the second girl.

QUESTION: When is it feasible or desirable to take on the judge in the lower court in the brief?

MR. KNAPP: When is it desirable to take on the misguided one who decided against you? Well, you always have to take him on, but you pretend that you never do. That is the simple answer to that question. That is where the phrase "the learned judge below" came from.

QUESTION: Before an appeal is taken, some lawyer has decided that it has merit and he has so advised his client. With that background, when you hear a more or less able lawyer appear before you as an appellant's counsel, you might have the presumption that this is a case that merits reversal, but somehow everybody on the panel seemed to accept the fact that the proclivity of the bench is going to be toward affirmance. That is very disrespectful to lawyers who have to advise their clients whether they should spend good money on an appeal or not.

Does the panel have an opinion on that?

JUDGE RIFKIND: Whether you recommend an appeal is one question. Whether you are going to win it is, of course, a totally different question. I mean that seriously. Whether to recommend an appeal may depend on the amounts at stake, the principle that you are establishing, its utility in other cases, all sorts of things of that kind. Whether the appeal is to be won is another matter.

Now, there seems to be, according to some of the questions, a notion that is incompatible with what I believe to be the appellate system in the Anglo-Saxon countries. With very few exceptions our appellate structure does not operate on a *de novo* system of trial. Generally speaking, you have a judgment. When you come into the appellate court, your position is, "This judgment is there, and it is now the law of this case." Obviously, you have the burden of persuading somebody to change it. You don't start afresh. You don't start on an even-Steven basis in the appellate court.

If you are the appellant, you have to persuade the court to change the lower court judgment. You have seen cases in which, at the conclusion of the appellant's argument, the court says, "There is no reason for listening to the respondent." That does not necessarily reflect on the appellant, nor does it mean any particular compliment to the respondent. It means that the burden hasn't been met.

I don't know why anybody should be surprised that in a very large percentage of the cases that burden will not be met, because there is a tremendous presumption in favor of the decision below.

References by Members of the Panel

CASES

Escobedo v Illinois (1964) 378 US 478
Memoirs of Hecate County (Doubleday & Company, Inc. v People of the State of New York) (1948) 335 US 848, *affirming* 297 NY 687, 77 NE2d 6, 272 App Div 799, 71 NYS2d 736
Miranda v Arizona (1965) 384 US 436

INDEX